ADHD

102 Practical Strategies for REDUCING THE DEFICIT

2nd Edition

By Kim "Tip" Frank, Ed.S., LPC
and
Susan J. Smith-Rex, Ed.D.

youth light
inc.

Illustrations by Walt Lardner
Layout and Design by Kimberly Grummond, Elizabeth Madden and Melissa Zace
Project Editing by Rebecca Van Gilder and Susan Bowman

ISBN 1-889636-36-3

Library of Congress Catalog Card Number 00-110475

10 9 8 7 6 5 4

Printed in the United States of America

For information address: YouthLight, Inc • P.O. Box 115 • Chapin, SC 29036 • 800-209-9774

Quantity orders may qualify for special terms.

Dedication

This book is dedicated to the many parents and professionals who are offering love, support and guidance to those who are affected by ADHD.

Table of Contents

There are many publications boasting 100 or 101 ideas or ways to accomplish something. With regard to <u>Attention Deficit Hyperactivity Disorder</u> there must be 100 or more ways to reduce the deficit. In fact, we have found 102 ways parents and professionals can help children and adolescents cope with and overcome ADHD.

Since ADHD is a chronic and pervasive condition, we have called this book "Reducing the Deficit." <u>Attention Deficit Disorders</u> don't <u>go away</u>, and their <u>effects can't be eliminated.</u> However, the <u>problems</u> that come with the <u>territory of ADHD can be greatly reduced.</u> ADHD is treatable and can be managed. We trust you will find our easy-to-understand information about ADHD and subsequent practical strategies very beneficial. We wish you success as you use them.

Kim "Tip" Frank, Ed.S., LPC

Susan J. Smith-Rex, Ed.D.

Section 1

UNDERSTANDING AND TREATING ADHD

The first section of our book is dedicated to providing useful information about attention disorders. From our perspective, ADHD is often misunderstood. We attempt to provide information in a simplistic, yet accurate way. Discussion on diagnosis, characteristics, and underlying causes is included, as well as ideas for explaining ADHD to others.

Treatment for ADHD is also carefully explained. We subscribe to a multimodal treatment plan. This form of treatment includes psychological counseling, educational planning, behavior modification, and medical management. All four of these modes of treatment are explained in great detail.

ADHD - ~~Multidal~~ multimodal treatment includes
1. psychological counseling
2. educational planning
3. behavior modification
4. medical management

Seven Keys to Understanding ADHD

You've no doubt heard many things about ADHD. There are many misconceptions about attention disorders. What a person with ADHD believes makes a huge difference when it comes to self-esteem and coping with life. People with ADHD have said things like:

"I'm dumb."

"I'm retarded."

"I'm lazy."

"I've got a brain disease."

"I'm just bad."

The fact is, people with ADHD are none of these things.

To the contrary, children, adolescents, and adults with ADHD are typically normal, healthy people. Instead of thinking of the ADHD person as "the problem," let's think of him/her as a person with a condition that is treatable. People with ADHD can and do learn skills to cope with their situation. This coping begins with an accurate understanding of ADHD.

1. Just What Do Those Four Letters Mean?

ADHD is an acronym that stands for Attention Deficit Hyperactivity Disorder. As early as in 1902, Dr. George Still identified students with ADHD characteristics. The term was first coined in 1980 by the American Psychological Association. Dr. Russell Barkley is often considered the Father of ADHD because of his research and writing on the condition. The *Diagnostic and Statistical Manual Fourth Edition* published by the American Psychiatric Association in 1994 breaks Attention Deficit Hyperactivity Disorder into three types.

Subtypes of ADHD

a. Predominantly inattentive type

b. Predominantly hyperactive-impulsive type

c. Combined type inattentive and hyperactive-impulsive

2. Five Key Elements in Defining and Diagnosing ADHD

ADHD is a medical diagnosis. When a physician (psychiatrist, neurologist, pediatrician, etc.) makes a diagnosis, he/she is looking at five criteria. If any one of the five don't fit the person's situation, a diagnosis of ADHD is not made. Much care should be taken before making a diagnosis. A careful look at the person's behaviors and family history are in order. Keep in mind there is no lab test used to diagnose ADHD.

The five diagnostic key elements are as follows:

a. **Chronic and pervasive** problems with inattention and/or impulsivity and/or hyperactivity

b. **Onset of symptoms** before age seven

c. **Symptoms** present across settings (e.g., at home, school, work, day care, etc.)

d. **Clear evidence** of interference with developmentally appropriate social, academic, or occupational functioning

e. **Symptoms** not accounted for by another mental disorder (e.g., Mood Disorder, Anxiety Disorder)

(Diagnostic & Statistical Manual, 4th edition)

3. Characteristics of ADHD

Professionals working with children and adolescents should be watchful for the characteristics of ADHD. Teachers and parents are often asked to fill out behavioral checklists such as the Conner's Scale or the ADDES. This information is an integral part of making a diagnosis.

a. Inattention

- Lack of attention to **details** - Doesn't seem to listen to what is being said

- **Careless** and **messy** work

- **Disorganization** - Often loses things necessary for tasks or activities at school or home

- Avoidance or dislike for **sustained activities** that require **mental effort**

- Failure to **follow through** or to **complete** tasks such as homework or chores

- Frequent **shifting** from one incomplete activity to another

- Difficulty in **completing tasks** - Easily distracted by extraneous stimuli

b. Hyperactivity

- **Fidgetiness** - inability to remain seated, squirms in seat, fidgets with hands and feet
- **Excessive activity** - talking, running, climbing
- Appearing **"driven by a motor"**
- **Noisy play** - -difficulty playing quietly

c. Impulsivity

- **Blurting** out answers
- Frequently **interrupting** or intruding on others
- **Difficulty taking turns** in games or group activities
- Doing **dangerous activities** without considering possible consequences

(Diagnostic & Statistical Manual, 4th edition)

4. Underlying Causes & Contributing Factors of ADHD

ADHD is a neurological condition. Think back to your days in biology class when you learned about how the central nervous system works. Your five senses take in information and send it to your brain.

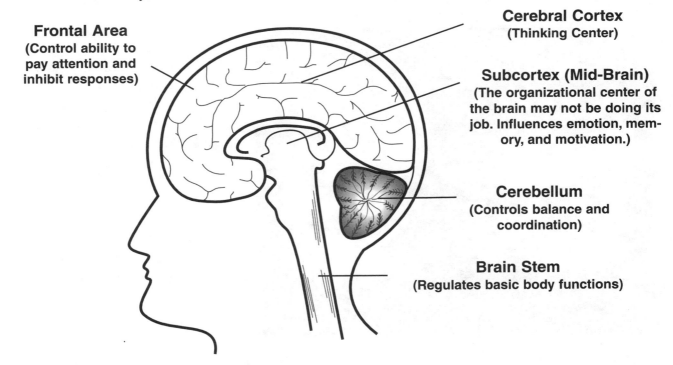

Frontal Area
(Control ability to pay attention and inhibit responses)

Cerebral Cortex
(Thinking Center)

Subcortex (Mid-Brain)
(The organizational center of the brain may not be doing its job. Influences emotion, memory, and motivation.)

Cerebellum
(Controls balance and coordination)

Brain Stem
(Regulates basic body functions)

These messages go to the **subcortex** or mid-brain. The subcortex is the relay system which helps send messages to the learning and thinking center **(cerebral cortex)**.

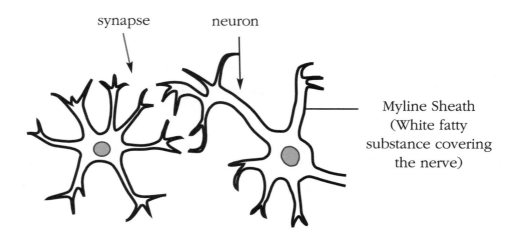

Messages are passed from one nerve cell **(neuron)** to the next. As pictured, there is a tiny space between each nerve cell called the **synapse**. Nerve cells relay messages across the synapse by chemical messengers called **neurotransmitters**.

Brain cells communicate by way of neurotransmitters. Researchers have identified 60 different neurotransmitters. For ADHD individuals, messages are not being sent quickly enough from neuron to neuron. This can be called a "filtering problem."

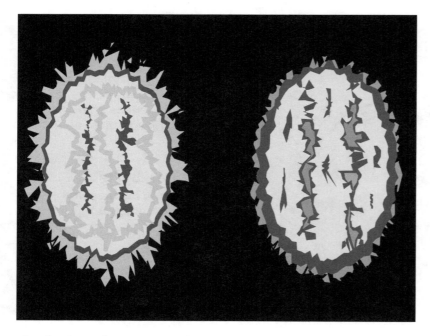

People with ADHD have low levels of certain chemical substances in the brain. **Note the picture which shows darker areas.** These darker areas represent a decrease in brain activity. The brain, having low levels of certain chemical substances, often needs to be strengthened through the use of medications which will be discussed later in this book.

In the March 18, 1996 issue of *Newsweek*, it was reported that the ADHD individual's brain may actually look different from a brain without ADHD. Through PET scans (Positron Emission Tomography) and MRIs (Magnetic Resonance Imaging), individuals with ADHD appear to have slightly smaller areas in the frontal lobe and less glucose, energy for the brain. Evidence indicates that there is possibly less electrical energy and less blood flow. This may explain the breakdown in goal-directed behavior and the ability to self-regulate. Babies are born with all of their brain cells but with few connections, called synapses, between the cells. The connections are forged by the experiences and stimulation that a baby receives. If neurons are used they are integrated. Unstimulated neurons will die. For this reason, early childhood stimulation is very important. The critical period is birth to 12.

a. Scope of Problem

Three to five percent of the school age population has an attention disorder. Males are diagnosed with ADHD much more often than females. In the general population, the ratio of ADHD males to ADHD females is 4 to 1. In clinical settings, those receiving help for ADHD, the ratio is 9 males to 1 female (Diagnostic & Statistical Manual, 4th edition).

b. Historical Relationships to ADHD

There is no known cause of ADHD. As mentioned earlier, there is evidence that bio-chemical imbalances within the brain are likely the source. There are, however, seven historical relationships where the ADHD conditions tends to be more prevalent, according to the *Diagnostic and Statistical Manual IV, (DSM IV)*:

- Neurotoxin exposure (e.g., lead poisoning)
- Infections (e.g., encephalitis)
- Drug exposure in utero
- Low birth weight
- Mental retardation
- Child abuse or neglect
- Multiple foster placements

There is also evidence of a hereditary link. There is a higher prevalence of ADHD in first degree biological relatives of children with ADHD. One half of children with ADHD have a parent with the disorder. One out of three children with ADHD have a sibling with the disorder (Diagnostic & Statistical Manual, 4th edition).

c. Other research on ADHD to consider

- Heredity explains 50 to 92 percent of hyperactive-impulsive behavior.
- At least 30 to 40 percent of children and adolescents with ADHD have relatives with the condition.
- A child is more likely to develop ADHD if the mother had complications before or during birth.
- Heredity may be a stronger factor than the complications (Barkley, 1995).

- Teratogens are substances that can block the normal development of a fetus, (maternal smoking, alcohol, drug abuse, nutrition, exposure to chemical poisons). Research indicates that certain teratogens increase the likelihood that a child will develop ADHD (Baren, 1994).

- ADHD seems to occur more often in the Unites States than other countries because of our genetic history. Our founding fathers were "risk takers" who came to America to start a new life. This may be a reason for a high gene pool of impulsive, curious individuals. (Hallowell and Ratey, 1995).

- Cultural Issues in Diagnosis

  Hispanic students, especially those from Puerto Rico, often display more body movements, gestures, and facial expressions than Anglo students do. Sometimes teachers who are not familiar with the culture will think they are hyperactive and inaccurately point to the student having ADHD (Bauermeister, 1995).

- Dr. Russell Barkley December, 1997 ADHD Report

  The severity of a child's level of ADHD symptoms has little to do with home environment or nutrition. Instead it has to do with the genetic endowments they gave their children at conception.

  This doesn't mean making changes doesn't benefit children but probably won't produce deep and sweeping changes.

  Parents are Shepherds not Engineers. (Barkley, 1998).

d. Behavioral Effects

Children and adolescents with ADHD are often considered lazy and irresponsible. The child with ADHD is sometimes perceived as oppositional defiant and the main problem within the family. These children can put a strain on family relationships. Another perception is that the child with ADHD is not intelligent. Because of learning problems and poor test taking skills, low I.Q. scores often occur. It is interesting to note that approximately 30% of ADHD children and adolescents also have a learning disability (CHADD, 1988). The DSM IV lists four behavioral effects.

- Strained family relationships
- Perception of laziness - poor sense of responsibility
- Oppositional Defiance
- Lower I.Q. scores

5. Major Concerns Students with ADHD Have About Themselves

Through our contact with hundreds of children with ADHD, a pattern of concerns held by these students has emerged. We have categorized these concerns into five areas. Incidentally, these discussions with students were the impetus behind our book *Getting A Grip on ADD: A Kid's Guide to Understanding and Coping With Attention Disorders* (Frank and Smith, 1994).

a. Poor Study Skills

Students expressed concerns about low grades. Students indicated that they didn't really know how to study and how to get organized.

b. Inability to Listen and Concentrate

Students felt they couldn't complete tasks and stay tuned into lessons.

c. Getting into Trouble at School and Home

Students indicated trouble making good decisions and an inability to control their behavior.

d. Unpleasant Feelings and Low Self-Esteem

Students expressed feelings such as anger, frustration, and powerlessness. Many students said they didn't like themselves.

e. Lack of Friendships and an Inability to Get Along with Others

Students said that others didn't like them and they didn't seem to know why. They also reported regular conflicts with peers.

6. Explaining ADHD to Children and Adolescents

When explaining attention disorders to students, sensitivity, simplicity, and accuracy are essential. Most people, including adults, misunderstand this disorder. As previously mentioned, students often feel dumb, lazy, or bad. Nothing could be farther from the truth. When children and adolescents truly understand their situation, they find new hope and reassurance.

a. Two Key Ideas

1. **"It's not as hard as you think."** We try to get students to think again about their situation and realize it is not hopeless or impossible to deal with. One key is to understand ADHD and to learn some tricks or skills to better cope. We try to impress upon children that they have a wonderful ability to work out problems and situations. Tell the student, "It's not as hard as you think," and "we'll get through it as we work together."

2. **"It's a matter of perspective."** "How are you looking at your ADHD? Is it awful or something terrible? If you think this way, you are giving yourself 'muddy messages.'" Instead, "clear messages" are needed such as, "I can deal with it," or "It's not easy, but I can learn ways to cope." The more positive a person is, the better chance he/she can succeed. Let's face it, attitude, or the way we think about life, is always one thing we can control. It's a matter of perspective.

b. Sensitively-Worded Explanations for Children

First, it is important to emphasize that these children are normal and healthy. By providing clearly and simply stated information that explains ADHD, children are reassured that their condition is very treatable. We recommend that you explain that scientists believe their brain is low in certain chemical substances. Therefore, their brain is slow to react and may have a lessened ability to filter out important information coming into their brain from our five senses. Many children have real difficulties with concentration and self-control. Emphasize to the children that they are not the only ones who struggle with these problems.

It is helpful to explain that certain medications such as Ritalin® or Adderall® are given to replace needed chemicals in the brain. The brain is then accelerated and is better able to aid with concentration and self-control. Such medications are essentially "brain fuel." Medications prescribed by doctors help the brain work more efficiently.

The book, *Getting a Grip on ADD: A Kid's Guide to Understanding and Coping with Attention Disorders,* is useful in helping to provide a simple but accurate explanation of ADHD to children (Frank and Smith, 1994). Information is shared about the role of physicians, use of medications, and the basic chemical makeup of the brain. The book is geared for children in grades three through eight. For younger children, we recommend that you simply paraphrase the information while looking at the pictures.

c. Sensitively-Worded Explanations for Adolescents

Since teenagers can readily understand basic biology, go over the information on pages 5-6 called Underlying Causes of ADHD. Going over these pictures and ideas should bring about a good understanding of ADHD.

7. ADHD and the Law

Laws have played a major role in the history of educating special needs students. The 5th and 14th Amendments to the U.S. Constitution are the most important sources of Constitutional rights for the handicapped. Since the mid-70's, Congress has adopted several pieces of legislation whose purpose was to end discrimination against the handicapped and to improve educational and other services available to them. Three laws need to be highlighted because of the possible implications for attention disorders:

a. Section 504 of the Rehabilitation Act of 1973 (RA) is a statute, general in nature, administered by both the Department of Education and the Department of Health and Human Services. Section 504 is not a federal grant program; unlike the IDEA, it does not provide federal money to assist students with special needs. This statute is intended to prohibit discrimination and to impress upon recipients of federal funds that there is to be no discrimination against such persons.

b. The 1990 Individuals with Disabilities Education Act (IDEA), formerly called the Education for All Handicapped Children's Act of 1975, was passed to prohibit discrimination and to also ensure a free, appropriate education to those students diagnosed as needing special education. IDEA, Public Law (105-17) was reauthorized in 1997. Attention disorders did not appear in the initial stages of this legislation since the term ADHD was first coined in 1980 when the *Diagnostic and Statistical Manual of Mental Disorders (DSM) III* was published. IDEA is administered by the U.S. Department of Education.

In 1991, the U. S. Department of Education issued a memorandum to state departments of education clarifying that students with attention deficit disorders may be eligible for special education under the category of "other health impaired". In instances where the ADHD is chronic and adversely affects educational performance and alertness, these students may be eligible for special education services.

If the ADHD student is categorized in special education as learning disabled or "other health impaired," the special educator is required to write an annual individualized education program (IEP). The components of the IEP are:

• the student's present levels of academic performance

• annual goals

• short-term instructional objectives

• related services

• duration of services

• transition plan (no later than age 14 and annually there after)

• plans for evaluation

An IEP is a written agreement between the parents, student, and school about what the child needs and what will be done to address those needs.

Should it be determined that the child with ADHD needs only adjustments in the regular classroom, rather than special education, those adjustments are required by law. This is called an Individualized Accommodations Plan (IAP). A range of strategies is available to meet the educational needs of children with ADHD. Regular and special classroom teachers play an important role in identifying and using appropriate educational adaptations and interventions for children with ADHD.

We trust that the **102** strategies and accommodations provided in Section Two and Three of this book will prove helpful in meeting the objectives of an IEP or an IAP.

c. The Americans with Disabilities Act (ADA) was passed in 1990 for the purpose of ending discrimination against individuals in the areas of employment, education, and public accommodations. Parents, teachers, and students need to be aware of these laws and their rights. Law is important, but it is only one factor in filling the needs of the ADD student.

Multimodal Treatment Plan

While there is no cure for ADHD, it is very treatable. Many people look at medication as the primary way to treat ADHD. While medications such as Ritalin® have proven to be helpful with 70% to 80% of those with ADHD (CHADD, 1988), a more well-rounded treatment plan is necessary. There is simply no "magic pill." The costs of not treating ADHD are sometimes high. Some possible effects are:

* Those untreated are more likely to become alcoholics, smokers, or drug abusers. (25% of the general adult population smoke, 40-60% of the the ADHD population smoke).

* More than 1/3 drop out of school.

* 1 out of every 10 ADHD adults attempts suicide.

People with ADHD need to learn coping skills, and the proper environment must be set at home and at school to make for success. We call this "covering all the bases." Consider the suggestions under each "base."

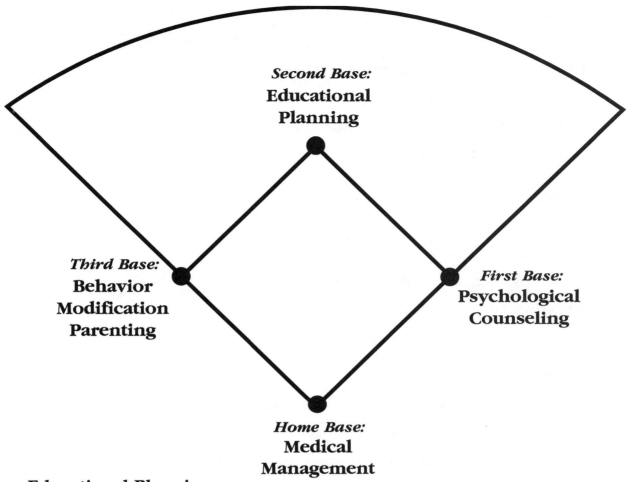

Second Base:
Educational
Planning

Third Base:
Behavior
Modification
Parenting

First Base:
Psychological
Counseling

Home Base:
Medical
Management

a. Educational Planning

It is a good idea to have a thorough psychoeducational evaluation done. This can be accomplished most economically through the school system. It can also be done through a private agency. Possible learning disabilities can be detected in this evaluation. Also, information gained from testing can be used for better instruction to meet each child's specific needs. A plan of action on the school's part to meet individual needs is often necessary. On pages 11-12, Individualized Education Plans (IEPs) and Individualized Accommodations Plans (IAPs) are discussed along with the legal aspects which schools must follow. Classroom modifications which we have found to be helpful for ADHD students are:

Setting the classroom environment

- Establish a stimuli-reduced study area

- Allow for peer tutoring (study buddy)

- Surround with good role models

- Give thought to the seating arrangement (near teacher's desk, in front of class, away from distracting stimuli, etc.)

- Keep a regular schedule, avoiding transitions and disruptions
- Make directions short and clear (avoid multiple commands)
- Get eye contact when directions are given
- Have student repeat directions before starting task
- Encourage student to ask questions and to seek assistance when needed
- Use an assignment folder or notebook signed by teacher

Discuss suggestions for staying on task

- Give only one task at a time
- Monitor frequently
- Modify assignments as needed
- Reduce length of assignments
- Provide extra time to complete tasks

Make recommendations for supervision and discipline

- Set pre-established rules and consequences for misbehavior
- Make consistent enforcement of rules
- Use a calm approach with consequences immediately enforced
- Use positive discipline without ridicule or sarcasm
- Praise good behavior and performance
- Provide rewards to shape positive behaviors

b. Behavioral Approaches to Parenting

Structuring the environment at home can reduce stress for the family. All children, especially those with ADHD, need a predictable environment. The simpler the lifestyle, the better. Warmth, appropriate involvement, and consistency are keys. The following are a few ideas that we've found helpful to make home a nicer place in which to live.

Encourage organizational skills

- Set clear priorities (don't over schedule)
- Break down tasks into fewest steps possible

- Organize child's room by providing bins, hooks, picture labels (provide diagrams of room as it should be organized to guide in cleanup)

- Provide a stimuli-free study area with needed materials organized

- Keep to a regular schedule

- Establish a routine to prepare for the next morning

- Use a reward system (charting desired behaviors)

Set age-appropriate expectations and use positive discipline

- Make accommodations but do not excuse from normal expectations

- Use simple but systematic approach to discipline (*1-2-3 Magic* Program by Dr. Thomas Phelan works well with ADHD ages 3-12. The videotape can be ordered at 1-800-44 CHILD.)

- Use a time-out area

- Stay positive (no name calling or verbal/physical abuse)

- Compliment tasks well-done

- Take dangerous objects away

- Encourage play with one or two friends (not large groups)

- Take away privileges for misbehavior

- Write assigned chores or tasks (job list or contract)

- Talk to the child in a room with few distractions (hold chin)

Encourage activities that build self-esteem and confidence

- Involve the child in social activities (scouts, church groups, etc.)

- Consider activities (bowling, karate, swimming, etc.)

- Use the computer for school work

- Teach child cognitive restructuring (positive self-talk)

- Provide a tutor

- Use social and organizational skills classes

- Allow the child to play with younger children if that is where they "fit in"

c. Psychological Counseling

Counseling is a crucial component of treatment. Gaining a healthy understanding of ADHD and learning how to cope are essential for success. The following are goals for good counseling.

- Educate the child about ADHD

- Focus therapy on giving the child skills to better cope with ADHD

- Use an active and direct approach (play therapy)

- Involve parents and educators in treatment

- Focus on ADHD issues such as study skills, listening skills, self-esteem, feelings, friendship, social skills, and behavior/self-control.

d. Medical Management

Many physicians use combinations of several medications, each intended to stimulate production of a different chemical in the brain. For example, a psychostimulant such as Dexedrine® may help with attentiveness but not with hyperactivity or impulsiveness. Antihypertensives such as Clonidine® or Tenex® may help with hyperactivity while antidepressants such as Prozac® or Wellbutrin® may cut down impulsiveness.

2. Rule of Thirds

It is believed that the majority of children with ADHD will no longer need medication when they are adults. This does not mean they have outgrown ADHD. Instead, they have learned enough coping skills that medication is no longer necessary. Some, however, just seem to require the medication to function more efficiently and effectively at work and in relationships.

Out of an average population of children taking medication in elementary school, nearly a third will no longer need it as they get into adolescence (Klein, 1987). As this population moves into adulthood, approximately another third will no longer need medication. This, of course, leaves just one-third still using medication for ADHD in their adult lives. The following is a summary of the types of medications most often used with ADHD.

3. Medications Used to Treat ADHD

Medication can be to an ADHD student as glasses are to a nearsighted person. Stimulants have been used since the late 1930's, with no known evidence of long term damage. Side effects are not usually serious in nature but need to be monitored by physicians.

a. Psychostimulants

- *Methylphenidate (Ritalin®)*
  - 20-40 mg per day
  - Two or three daily doses, unless sustained release form (then one or two doses)
  - Drug effect typically lasts three to four hours
  - Drug effect occurs within 15 minutes
  - Best given after meals
  - Possible side effects are gastrointestinal problems, palpitations, hypertension, dry mouth, insomnia, anorexia, depression, and stunted growth in children

- *Dextroamphetamine (Dexedrine®) or Methamphetamine (Desoxyn®)*
  - 10-30 mg per day
  - Two to three daily doses
  - Drug effect lasts two to six hours
  - Drug effect occurs within 15 minutes
  - Best given after meals
  - Possible side effects are gastrointestinal problems, palpitations, hypertension, dry mouth, insomnia, anorexia, depression, and stunted growth in children

- *Pemoline (Cylert®)*
  - 37.5 to 75 mg per day
  - Usually start at 37.5 mg per day and increase weekly by 18.75 mg until therapeutic effect occurs
  - One daily dose
  - Therapeutic effect may take six to eight weeks
  - Possible side effects are gastrointestinal problems, palpitations, hypertension, dry mouth, insomnia, anorexia, depression, and stunted growth in children

- *Adderall (A combination of medications including Dextroamphetamine Saccharate®, Dextro-amphetamine Sulfate®, Amphetamine Aspartate®, and*

Amphetamine Sulfate®)

- 10 to 30 mg per day
- Drug effect lasts approximately three hours
- Drug effect occurs within 15 minutes
- Best given after meals
- Possible side effects are insomnia, stomach pain, headache, irritability, and weight loss (As with most psychostimulants indicated for ADHD, there is the possibility of growth suspension and the potential for precipitating motor tics.)

b. Antidepressants

- Tricyclics - imipramine (Tofranil®), desipramine, and nortriptyline
- Bupropion (Wellbutrin®)
- Monoamine oxidase inhibitors
- Fluoxetine (Prozac®)

c. Antihypertensives:

- Clonidine (Catapres®)
- Beta-blockers (Inderal®, Tenormin®)
- Tenex

d. Areas of Impairment/Effective Medical Treatment

- Inattention/Distractibility - Psychostimulant (affects dopamine)
- Impulsivity - Prozac® (affects serotonin)
- Hyperactivity - Tricyclics/Beta Blockers/Clonidine (affects adrenaline)

4. Medical Management Problems

Although medications can be very helpful for children, there are several issues that need to be considered. Medications are most effectively used when monitored by a physician, who is given regular feedback from parents, teachers, and children. Problems occur when parents control the drug without consulting a physician. Keep in mind that medications often lose some of their effectiveness when used over a long period of time. For this reason, physicians often suggest a break from medication, especially in the summer, or a change in the medication prescribed. Sometimes parents assume that the medication is no longer useful and discontinue its use.

Another problem, especially with pre-teens and adolescents, is their resistance to taking medication. Because of their belief about being perceived as looking different, along with any bothersome side effects, they often decide that medication is of no benefit. Helping the preteen or teen see the benefits of taking medications as prescribed is necessary to enlisting his/her support.

Medication Saboteurs
Factors that Diminish the Effectiveness of Medication

Medication is subject to a healthy sense of guardedness...unfortunately, some people may become easily alarmed and over react when they hear an offhand remark, or see a brief article in the the newspaper.

"The answer is in this little pill..."

The adult's attitudes are shown by voice tone, choice of words,
e.g., "Look at you! You must not have taken your medication today."
Other kids may tease or taunt you for taking medication

Antibiotics for the Saboteurs

Self-monitoring of behavior

Self-monitoring of your response to medication

Teaching assertiveness skills and communication skills to enhance direct communication with the doctor

Providing accurate information to the person who takes the medication

Promoting student ownership: understanding, acceptance, compliance, evaluation

Adapted with permission from *Creative Strategies for Working With ODD Children and Adolescents* by Frank, Paget, Bowman, and Smith-Rex (1998) YouthLight, Inc.

Section 2

STRATEGIES AND ACCOMMODATIONS FOR SCHOOL AND HOME

This section focuses on a selection of strategies or approaches to help students, teachers, and parents foster educational success. Regular educational classrooms contain substantial numbers of students with diverse learning needs. Many of these students display characteristics that can significantly interfere with successful learning. These factors can result from factors such as language differences, varied cognitive abilities, behavior, medical needs, or limited experiential backgrounds. Many of these at-risk students require special attention, however, only some of them require special education. Sometimes modifications of the physical dimensions of the classroom, classroom management strategies, school and family collaboration techniques, and innovative study skills and social skills can provide the boundaries needed for students to achieve success.

Accommodations and Strategies for School

The following are **102** useful classroom accommodations and strategies for students with ADHD. Also included are worksheets that can be photocopied and used immediately at school and at home.

1. Strategic Seating

It is very important for teachers to systematically consider the best seating assignment and arrangement for every student in the classroom. Most ADHD students benefit from a location that:

- Is away from visual and auditory distractions.

- Has good natural light.

- Is near a study buddy who is a mature role model.

- Is in close proximity to the teacher.

- Has a storage area (a basket cubby, locker, etc.) that assists with organization.

2. Reinforcers and Consequences

Classroom rules should always be carefully explained to students and parents, be clearly posted, and used consistently and quickly.

Consider Lee Canter's *Assertive Discipline Approach* (Canter, 1982) or Dr. Thomas Phelan's *1-2-3 Magic* (Phelan, 1984). Both systems are based on a systematic approach utilizing basic behavior modification principles. The programs focus generally on two things: how to stop negative behaviors (stop behaviors), and how to start positive behaviors (start behaviors). The success of the program hinges upon reducing the amount of talk and emotion expended by the adult in charge. Immediate and consistent consequences or rewards are provided. This in turn shapes the desired behaviors.

Other ideas to consider are explained below:

- Enforce consequences fairly, quickly and consistently.

- Stick to a regular class routine, (for the most part).

21

- Establish a procedure that allows frequent, structured breaks.

- Use activities such as running errands to help students relax and refocus.

- Give the student a prescribed number of passes to move around the room or school (boundaries or limits are usually helpful). When the passes are used, the student must remain seated.

- Change positive reinforcers fairly often to maintain and stimulate interest.

- Administer a reinforcement inventory to determine interests.

The following reproducible reinforcement inventory can provide information about which specific reinforcers are considered valuable to a particular child.

Reinforcement Inventory

Name _____ Date _____

1. When you have free time outside of school, what do you like to do most? _____
    _____

2. List three of your favorite foods.
    _____, _____, _____

3. Name three games you like to play.
    _____, _____, _____

4. Write down the names of your favorite singers or bands.
    _____, _____, _____

5. Do you like to read as a hobby?_____ Name a favorite book._____

6. List something you like to do with your:

        Parents,   Sister/Brother,   Best Friend,

    _____, _____, _____

7. What would you like to do when you are an adult?
    _____

8. When you have some money what do you like to do?
    _____

9. If you had a free day, what would you like to do?
    _____

10. Which movies and TV programs do you enjoy?
    _____

11. What are your favorite hobbies?
    _____

12. What are your favorite activities or places to go?

    _____   _____

    _____   _____

    _____   _____

3. Multimodal Learning

Use different creative techniques to stimulate the senses and increase attention.

Learning takes place when information is processed through our five basic senses (seeing, hearing, touching, tasting and smelling). By incorporating a multi-modal approach of stimulating various senses during the learning process, chances increase that material will be better understood, remembered longer and later retrieved.

As a teacher, your job is to systematically observe and determine which senses or modes of learning are strongest for each student. Discuss your observations with each student and consider using a multi-modal approach when planning lessons. Consider, for example, the VAKT Approach.

The VAKT Approach to Instruction

Students learn all material and tasks by processing information through their senses. Grace Fernald's VAKT technique (Visual, Auditory, Kinesthetic, Tactile) can be adapted to all learning objectives, to allow multi-modal processing to occur.

When planning lessons, teachers should consider procedures which will enable students to process information through more than one of the senses. Using this technique, learning will become more stimulating and hopefully be retained longer.

Consider the following suggestions:

a. Say the words, count the letters or syllables, talk about the size or patterns of letters during spelling or rote memory tasks.

b. Write words in sand, sandpaper, finger paint, shaving cream, or rolled out clay to stimulate the tactile sense.

c. Rehearse objectives to promote success with memory. Students are to indicate when they are ready to write or recite without a model. When needed, students are to study again. More attempts may be needed to yield a smooth, automatic reproduction.

d. Use olfactory (smell) and gustatory (taste) senses when appropriate to the lesson.

e. Use visual aids throughout each lesson.

f. Encourage the use of a tape recorder, a computer and oral reports as alternative methods for student responses.

g. Read assignments aloud when appropriate. When reading for comprehension, read, stop and draw a picture. Mind mapping increases comprehension (see page 57).

(Fernald, 1943)

4. Flexible Testing

Consider flexible time restrictions and methods for test administration for ADHD students. Stress quality not quantity. For example:

a. Review old tests to allow familiarity with a teacher's format.

b. Allow more time if needed for students to complete the test.

c. Allow the students to take the test on a computer.

d. Allow the students to take the test orally.

e. Provide an opportunity for take home tests when appropriate.

5. Tools for Organization

Students can greatly benefit from time-management schedules and organizational tools at home and school. The examples which follow can provide weekly structure.

Homework Folder

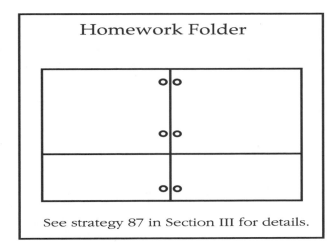

See strategy 87 in Section III for details.

Notebook

3 ring notebook with:

- Dividers for each subject
- Homework folder inserted
- Class schedule reminder sheet

Desk

Provide basket under chair for extra materials not needed for class.

Locker

Vertically place books in order of class day. Color code book jackets.

1st	2nd	3rd	4th	5th	6th

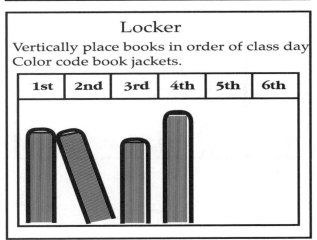

Home Schedule

Week of_____   Name_____

	Monday	Tuesday	Wednesday	Thursday	Friday
Before School					
After School					
Evening					

List activities and tasks that need to be done for each part of the day during the school week.

Homework Assignments

Week of_____   Name_____

Teacher Signature _____

Parent Signature _____

- In the first column, write down the subject or class.
- Write down all assignments for each day.
- Teacher signs to ensure assignments are recorded accurately.
- Parent signs to ensure assignments are done satisfactorily.

Subject/Class	Monday	Tuesday	Wednesday	Thursday	Friday
_____					
_____					
_____					
_____					
_____					
_____					
_____					

Daily Requests or Assignments

1. _____
   _____

2. _____
   _____

3. _____
   _____

4. _____
   _____

5. _____
   _____

6. _____
   _____

7. _____
   _____

8. _____
   _____

9. _____
   _____

10. _____

We encourage you to use pages 28-30 as a unit to encourage improved follow-through on assignments and tasks. This is a simple three step approach for planning ahead. Please follow the directions below.

- Make several copies of this sheet.

- List all requests or assignments each day on one sheet.

- Put a star beside those which are most urgent.

- Scratch them off your list once you have completed them.

- If anything is still on your list at the end of the day, transfer it either to the monthly calendar or the daily plan sheet for the next day (See pages 29 and 30).

- Try to complete all requests or assignments before going to bed or move it to the monthly calendar.

Monthly Calendar

Month _____

Fill in the dates.

Monday	Tuesday	Wednesday	Thursday	Friday	Sat./Sun.
__	__	__	__	__	__ / __
__	__	__	__	__	__ / __
__	__	__	__	__	__ / __
__	__	__	__	__	__ / __
__	__	__	__	__	__ / __

Daily Plan Sheet

AM	PM
7:00	1:00
8:00	2:00
9:00	3:00
10:00	4:00
11:00	5:00
12:00	6:00
	7:00
	8:00
	9:00
	10:00

6. Direction Words

Instructions should be simply stated and written on the board. Students are to write down each assignment on their homework assignment sheet (see page 27). Direction words should be reviewed in order to make sure students can read and understand required tasks. Underline each direction with a different color to alert students to follow the sequence of directions.

Direction Words

Make sure students can read and understand the task required for the following direction words: (Brigance Inventory)

1st grade words

circle	draw	print
color	find	read
count	mark	show
cut	open	write

2nd grade words

choose	match	start
close	paste	trace
copy	place	turn
hold	put	underline

3rd grade words

bend	fold
check	follow
cross	list
divide	sign
touch	

4th grade words and beyond

complete	compare	discuss	outline
crease	contrast	evaluate	relate
measure	analyze	illustrate	summarize
select	define	interpret	
defend	diagram	justify	

7. Note-Taking Techniques

Taking notes in class is not an easy process. However, there are some strategies that can help the student stay more focused and attentive.

Box notes
Every 10 min

10 min

- Provide guided notes of the class lecture (see page 33), expect students to be active listeners by filling in the blanks.

- Require students to take notes in ten minute intervals where there are no guided notes provided. Students are held accountable for having key ideas written down every ten minutes (see pages 34-35). Students are expected to monitor their own behavior by listening and inserting lecture information in each box.

Examples of guided notes and ten minute interval note taking follow.

Guided NOTES

What You Should Know About Guided Notes

Guided notes are teacher-made handouts which "guide" a student during a lecture. Standard cues and specific spaces are provided to write key concepts, facts, and/or relationships. The idea behind guided notes is to take advantage of the research-based conclusion that youngsters who make responses often and appropriately during a lesson learn more than ones who are passive and uninvolved.

There are short-form guided notes and long-form guided notes. The short-form guided notes require students to fill in blanks with single words or short phrases. Long-form guided notes require students to write the key concept/idea in sentences or phrases.

Located on the next page is an example of short-form guided notes.

Ocean Facts

In case you were wondering why earth is called the "water planet," consider these percentiles.

_____ % of the earth is covered with water

_____ % of that water is salt water

_____ % is fresh water

The four largest oceans in order of size are:

1. P_____
2. A_____
3. I _____
4. A_____

The world's deepest ocean is the _____ which has a maximum depth of _____ feet.

Scientists estimate that there are at least _____ _____ that live in the oceans.

Water temperatures vary greatly, from _____ to _____.

Water is composed of _____ and _____. In addition, there are 44 elements in sea water.

Name at least five elements found in sea water.

_____

_____

10 Minute Note Taking

Subject: _____

Date: _____

Name: _____

10 minutes

10 minutes

Note: Please see page 32 for directions.

10 minutes

10 minutes

10 minutes

8. "Study Pal" Notes

It is often helpful to pair ADHD students with a classroom study pal. When possible, allow the ADHD student to photocopy or carbon-copy their study pal's notes. The teacher can also provide a copy of his/her presentation notes. Keep in mind that we are not trying to frustrate the student, but rather to teach important information.

9. Skimming

Teach students how to skim and scan paragraphs for key words and main ideas. Teach the multi-pass strategy (see Strategy 10). If students enjoy reading lower grade level books but are sensitive about being criticized, a colorful book jacket could discourage peer teasing.

Skimming is rapid reading for facts. Whenever it is necessary to find specific facts in a paragraph, look very quickly at sentences which provide the information needed. When you skim reading information by the page or paragraph, you are quickly examining sentences for answers to questions you have (Weiner and Bazerman, 1982). When you skim you:

- Know exactly what information you are seeking. Question yourself about the information.

- Quickly move your eyes from line to line and from sentence to sentence.

- Stop when you think you've found the information that you were seeking.

- Slowly read the exact part of the line or lines that tells you the answer to what you are seeking, the question you asked.

- Think about the question for which you were finding an answer.

- Ask yourself, "Were you able to answer the question with the information you found?"

- Write down the answer to the question you were asked without wasting time.

10. Multi-Pass Strategy

The *Multi-Pass Strategy* (Deshler, 1984) encourages students to pass through a reading assignment a multitude of times, even if it isn't read word for word. When a student skims reading material, it is generally to obtain an impression or general overview of the content. Students are taught to look for information which is critical for comprehension of the content and be better prepared for lectures and discussion which will follow. Students are asked to pass through their assignment a multitude of times to gather major points. For example, the students may be asked to:

- Read questions at the end of the chapter

- Read all major headings

36

- Read every picture, chart or graph
- Define italicized words in their notes (use glossary if he/she needs it)

11. Immediate Feedback *— Pair up with study Pal to ck HWK*

Teachers need to be prompt in returning homework and assignments. Often pairing up with a study pal to check homework saves the teacher time and gives instant feedback to the students.

12. Class Reminders

Teach students to regularly review their "class reminder checklist" before entering each class. Students should keep this checklist in the front of their notebooks. The following is an example of a "class reminder checklist."

Class Reminder Checklist

Before class: Make sure you have the necessary materials:

_____ books   _____ notebook
_____ homework assignment   _____ paper
_____ pencil   _____ special materials: dictionary, ruler, compass

When class begins: Make sure you are seated before the bell rings.

Be quiet and attentive with materials ready.

During class: Make sure you are paying attention.

Take notes for every 10 minute period.

Participate and ask questions.

Distract no one.

End of class: Write down assignment.

Make sure you take home books and materials.

Set up an appointment to get extra assistance if needed.

Prepare for your next class.

---

13. Homework Checklist for Parents

It is a common belief that students who spend one hour per day doing homework usually pass their courses. Sometimes parents need to monitor and reward daily effort. Try using the homework checklist for parents that follows for a nine-week grading period and see if it makes a difference.

Homework/Study Time

Week	Monday	Tuesday	Wednesday	Thursday	Total
1.					
2.					
3.					
4.					
5.					
6.					
7.					
8.					
9.					

Directions for Homework Checklist for Parents:

1. Fill in the dates for a nine-week grading period down the left column.

2. Decide on Sunday evening what reward the student will be working to earn during the upcoming week. Share ideas for this reward with the student.

3. Give one point for each 30 minutes spent on homework each day.

4. Total the points earned for the week on Thursday nights.

5. Give rewards or privileges for seven or more points earned per week.

14. Daily Communications

Teachers communicating with parents on a daily or weekly basis can be very beneficial to help ADHD students stay on task and take more responsibility for actions and decisions. Daily or weekend privileges should be based on school effort. Two examples follow, one for elementary and one for middle school, in which the teacher is asked to provide daily feedback to the parents.

Teacher Comment Sheet for the Elementary Age Student

Communicating Daily with Parents

	Name _____
	Target Behavior _____

	Yes	No
Monday	_____	_____
Tuesday	_____	_____
Wednesday	_____	_____
Thursday	_____	_____
Friday	_____	_____

Directions to Parents:

1. Use index cards to make the above example on a weekly basis.

2. Give your child a card every Monday morning.

3. Have teacher initial the appropriate box at the end of each school day. Provide the agreed daily reward only if the student brings home the card and if the teacher's initials are in the yes box.

4. Make an objective decision each day by having the teacher stack colored blocks or place colored beads in a jar every 30 minutes. Green - good; Red - not good. At the end of the day, the higher stack answers the question of whether the initial is yes or no.

Teacher Comment Sheet for Middle School

Student's name _____

Week of _____

Subject: _____

Teacher's Signature_____

Comments:

Assignments: _____

Subject: _____

Teacher's Signature_____

Comments:

Assignments: _____

Subject: _____

Teacher's Signature _____

Comments:

Assignments: _____

Subject: _____

Teacher's Signature _____

Comments:

Assignments: _____

15. Self-Monitoring and Personal Prescriptions

Self-monitoring by the student, whether it be academic or behavioral performance, can often be effectively achieved through the use of a personal prescription. The student and teacher together develop the self-monitoring prescription by discussing which behaviors, if changed, could enable the student to better achieve school success and be accepted by peers. Stress that it is important to always aim for a target. If a person has a goal, then he/she is likely to hit it. Prescriptions are checklists that the student reviews during the day and rates him/herself periodically as to the effort being exerted. The following sheets give examples of different personal prescriptions. The first example is a series of questions written by the teacher for the student to read throughout the day. The student is only expected to think about what was discussed earlier and attempt to follow the requests.

Name _____

1. Am I in my seat?

2. Do I have the materials I need out?

3. Am I talking to or touching anyone?

4. Am I listening to the teacher?

5. Did I write down my assignment for tomorrow?

Here is a blank prescription form to be completed for each individual student:

Name _____

1.

2.

3.

4.

5.

Self-Monitoring of Work and Behavior for Primary Children or Nonreaders

This prescription works best when teachers want students to work independently and monitor behaviors which need improvement. A card is taped on a child's desk daily. The card shown on the next page is an example for primary level students or youngsters who are nonreaders. The student is to go to the learning center marked by the circle and complete the activity. After completing each activity, students give themselves one point for accomplishing that activity and one point for accomplishing each behavior (then move to Activity 2 and 3).

Daily Self-Monitoring Card - Taped on the desk

Daily Self-Monitoring Card

	Points
Activity 1:	_____
No yelling	_____
Stay in seat	_____
Activity 2:	_____
No yelling	_____
Stay in seat	_____
Activity 3:	_____
No yelling	_____
Stay in seat	_____
Total:	_____

If appropriate, the student counts the number of points given at the end of the day. The teacher and student discuss at break time whether the student's perception of effort matches the teacher's impression. It has been our experience that when the student is involved in the rating process, effort does increase.

Rewards are then given.

Self-Monitoring of Work and Behavior for Primary Children or Nonreaders

This is a blank prescription for teachers to individualize with students. On the following page is an example of a task sheet that breaks up the entire school day into set intervals for students to monitor their behavior and work completion.

Daily Self-Monitoring - Taped on the desk

Activity 1: _____

Activity 2: _____

Activity 3: _____

Total: _____

Rewards or privileges are earned by students when the desired number of points are attained.

Task Sheet

Student: _____ Week of: _____ Observer: _____

	M	T	W	Th	F	Comments
1. Unpack books quietly						
2. Return Homework						
3. Complete Journal						
4. Activity Class						
5. Lunch						
6. Bathroom and Hall Behavior						
7. Story or Game Time						
8. Nap						
9. Recess						
10 Center time - Independently						
11. Work time - with teacher						
12. Pack and Leave Time						
TOTALS						

16. The Cueing Strategy

Staying focused and being able to use time wisely are important behaviors. Sometimes the use of hand signals between student and teacher can assist attention deficit students in developing and improving in these behaviors. Students' names do not need to be spoken for others to hear, and there is something very special about one-to-one communication. It can be motivating, soothing, and fun.

Teach your students the following signs and use them regularly.

Come: With your index fingers out, roll out hands towards your body.

Yes: Move your fist up and down in front of you.

Quiet: Begin with your finger on your lips. Move hand down and away from the mouth.

Good: Place the tips of your fingers of your right hand on your chin and move your hand out to meet your left palm.

No: Bring your index and middle finger together in one motion to your thumb.

Stop: Chop your right hand into the palm of your left.

Sit Down: Both open hands are held palms down and fingers pointing forward. Move hands down a short distance.

Help: Close the left hand in fist. Lift the left hand with an open right hand.

Work: Both hands are made into fists. The right hand strikes the top of the left hand several times.

Try: Put your thumbs between your index and middle fingers. In a circular motion, touch your chest and push out.

Look: Point to your eyes, then twist your hand and point in the desired direction.

Line Up: Face palms of hands together. Move hands apart, right hand toward the chest and left outward.

(Frank and Smith, 1994)

17. Memory Techniques

Being able to remember a lot of school information for tests can be hard! However, knowing a few tricks can make the process less frustrating and hopefully even enjoyable. Consider a few of the following techniques:

a. **Mnemonics** is making up a clue to help memory. For example, to memorize the names of all of the world continents, take the first letter of each and make up a silly sentence which will become a clue word. For example:

   • List the continents: Africa, Antarctica, Australia, Europe, Asia, North America, South America

   • First letters are: AAAEANS (Clue Word)

   • Silly Sentence: Three ants eat apples North and South.

b. **Clustering information** is dividing the information to be learned into groups or clusters so a student can learn information quicker and easier. For example, if asked to name the capitals of the 50 states, alphabetize the states and divide the list into five clusters. Learn each cluster of 10 states and capitals before adding the second, third, etc.

c. **Visualization** involves looking at what is to be learned, closing one's eyes and mentally seeing the information.

d. **Visual rehearsal** involves putting information on index cards or notebook paper and reviewing it many times throughout the day. Once the student believes the spelling or order is remembered, then the student is to write it down from memory.

e. **Oral rehearsal** involves rehearsing over and over what is to be said. Practice can make perfect! The more repetitions and experiences, the easier the presentation can become.

f. **Listening for cue words** is training the student's ear for words that indicate the teacher thinks the information is important and should be remembered. Listen for words such as: "This is an important fact" or words like always, all, never, or don't forget. Other word categories that can "Signal" important information are:

1. Developing Categories	2. Cause & Effect	3. Time Order	4. Conclusions
First	*Because*	*After*	*Finally*
Second	*Consequently*	*Next*	*To Summarize*
Ordinal numbers		*Before*	

18. Assignment Order

It is not uncommon for the student to become overwhelmed when a lot of assignments and requests are handed out. This is when it is important to have students look closely at the Daily Request Sheet on page 28 and place a star beside the items which are most urgent to complete. The student is to work on these items first and then see how many of the others can be done. If time runs out, the student is to move those items not accomplished to the monthly calendar on page 29.

19. Math Manipulatives and Help Sheets

If needed, encourage students to use objects when completing computation assignments. If students are having difficulty memorizing the multiplication tables, prepare ditto sheets of the multiplication tables for the students to use so they are not penalized in learning other concepts. Consider making laminated class response cards to increase student engagement throughout lessons. The student holds up the card naming the operation being used.

+	-	X	÷

20. Finger trick for Multiplication: 6,7,8, and 9's

Objective: Students will be able to multiply facts using the numbers 6, 7, 8, and 9.

Often the higher facts in multiplication are difficult for students to memorize. This is a trick to use for multiplying facts using the numbers 6, 7, 8, and 9. The trick will not work for any factors less than 6. Both hands are used for this trick. Each finger is assigned a number on both hands.

index finger - 6   **ring finger - 8**

middle finger - 7   **pinky finger - 9**

Note: <u>Thumbs</u> are <u>ALWAYS</u> tucked in.

1. Hold up both hands with palms facing out. Put up the fingers needed for the problem and tuck the unused fingers down. For example, 8 x 9. On one hand all fingers to the 8 finger would be up and on the other hand, all fingers to the 9 finger would be up. The unused fingers remain tucked down.

2. Count the fingers that are up by tens.

3 fingers   +   4 fingers =   7 fingers x 10 = 70

3. Flip your hands around and multiply the fingers tucked down on each hand together.

2 x 1 = 2

4. Add the top and bottom.

70 + 2 = 72   **SO**   8 x 9 = 72

Copied with permission from Maureen S. Tiller, M.Ed, Director of Special Services, Laurens School District 56, Clinton SC 29325 (864) 833-0802

21. Pressure Point Technique

When feeling drowsy or distracted, try pushing your pressure points to regain focus on the lesson or task involved. With your thumb, moderately push the pressure point on your other forearm. The pressure point is found on the muscle area below your elbow. This also serves as a magic button to manage anger and frustration.

22. Scotopic Sensitivity

Individuals with reading difficulties may react differently to particular frequencies and wavelengths of the white light spectrum. Over sensitivity to certain frequencies of light may be a cause of reading difficulties. Some reading specialists recommend the use of colored overlays, selected by the student, to place over reading materials to increase one's ability to focus on the assignments given.

Strategies for Teachers Who Have a Student with Severe ADHD

One of the greatest challenges for teachers is managing children with special needs. The move toward "inclusion" makes it a necessity to have skills and confidence as you manage all types of students. The next strategies that follow include ideas for teachers dealing with a student with severe ADHD.

23. "Australia"

"Australia" is a good place for those horrible, terrible, no good, very bad days. Everyone (including teacher and student) needs a break when things are rapidly disintegrating. Therefore, a preestablished spot which is a stimuli-reduced zone is made available. The teacher cues the student that a trip to "Australia" is needed to refocus or to calm down. A student may also choose to move to "Australia" if he/she feels a need to get a grip on behavior or concentration.

"Australia" is placed in an area where the student can participate in the lesson but can also have some space from fellow students. A set of books and school supplies is provided so the student can complete classwork. In this work zone, the student also has more freedom to stand and move so long as he/she stays on task and doesn't bother others.

Please note, this area is available to all students. Therefore, the ADHD student is not singled out.

24. Listen, Look, and Think: Self-Monitoring On-Task Behavior

Intermittent reinforcement is the most effective type of reinforcement to shape positive behaviors. Staying on task while completing an assignment is a skill which requires much self-discipline and practice. Dr. Harvey Parker has put together a simple method to encourage on-task behavior. He has developed a continuous-play signaling tape and pad for self-recording. This reduces teacher (or parent) reminders to pay attention. The student self-monitors whether or not he/she was on task at the sound of the beep on the tape. Classical conditioning is in effect here. The student associates the tone with being on task, and with practice, the student learns to sustain attention for longer periods of time.

To order *Listen, Look, and Think* contact the A.D.D. Warehouse, Plantation Florida.

25. "Pre-Mac" Your Day

We all look forward to a break. McDonald's restaurant some time ago had a very effective commercial and jingle called "You deserve a break today." Something about rewarding yourself just makes life worth living.

One effective method for helping students to stay on task is to combine continuous time on task with short breaks. The teacher and student can set realistic goals in terms of time on task and the amount of work to be done during an interval of time.

26. The Turtle Technique

This technique is primarily used for young children who tend to be aggressive. It involves using the code word "turtle." This code word cues or prompts the child to stop negative behavior and think about his/her behavior. The child is trained to "crawl into his/her shell." Young children are trained to find a seat or corner and bunch up into a ball with hands over the head. This position is similar to the position used in a tornado drill. The child, of course, pretends he/she is a turtle who has crawled into his/her shell.

Older elementary age students may opt to use the cue or code word "turtle" as a signal to simply sit in a chair. While in the "shell," the child is trained to relax. This can be as simple as taking a deep breath and thinking about what to do. On the other hand, students can be taught muscle relaxation techniques. The child stays in his/her shell until he/she is calm and in control.

27. Enlist Support of Class

One much overlooked idea for classroom management is to gain the understanding and support of the students in the classroom. The ADHD student is frequently viewed with disdain by fellow students. Before a negative attitude emerges, it may be wise to call a "class meeting" without the ADHD student present. Perhaps the ADHD student can be sent to run an errand or to do a particular activity outside of class. The teacher then explains the need for everyone to help out. The teacher may matter of factly explain that the particular student is having difficulty with self-control and/or concentrating on school work. Explain that these behaviors may be frustrating at times and emphasize the need to not get "emotionally hooked" or overly upset about inappropriate behavior. Instruct classmates to ignore inappropriate behaviors as much as possible. Also, teach students assertiveness skills. A separate lesson which includes practicing "I" messages would be time well spent. Note the following steps and examples:

> A. Say the person's name . . . "Sam,"
>
> B. Tell how you feel . . . "I feel frustrated. . ."
>
> C. Tell why . . . "when you don't help our group."
>
> D. Tell what you want . . . "Please do your part."

Strategies for Teachers Who Have Several Students with ADHD

It does not always follow that three to five percent of the students in a classroom are diagnosed with ADHD. It would make sense that one or two students would proportionally fall into a given classroom. "Murphy's Law," however, would allow far more than the normal number of ADHD students to land in a classroom. A teacher in this situation needs some helpful strategies.

28. Divide and Conquer

Separate students who have ADHD and surround them with positive role models. ADHD students tend to distract each other. As mentioned in Strategy 1, strategic seating of students affords opportunities for peer tutoring and positive peer pressure. The time used to develop a class sociogram is well worth it.

29. Token Economy

Token economies can be used very effectively in a classroom with several students who have ADHD. In this system tokens are earned for specific positive behaviors. (e.g., completing work on time, working quietly, etc.). Tokens are exchanged for backup rewards such as privileges and tangible objects. Creative teachers have set up a system where weekly paychecks are given. Savings accounts can also be used. A token economy can be set up as shown on the following page:

a. Identify a few target behaviors to reward.

- At most, choose three specific behaviors.

- State the behaviors in specific terms and word them positively. (e.g., staying on task, following directions, completing homework)

b. Choose type of tokens to be used (e.g., poker chips, cards, stamps, stickers, points, play money, etc.).

c. Determine the backup rewards. Use a number of privileges or tangible objects that tokens can buy.

d. Determine the token values for target behaviors.

   • Token values can be weighted according to the difficulty of the task, or each behavior may be worth one token.

e. Determine purchase price or number of tokens for rewards.

   • Initially, make rewards very attainable.

   • Gradually increase expectations to earn rewards.

   • Utilize daily and weekly rewards.

It is motivational for students to see their progress. A chart or graph keeping track of tokens earned should be displayed. Provide feedback to the students at the end of each day.

One other possibility is to remove tokens for inappropriate behaviors such as fighting with peers or backtalking to teacher.

Cautions: This system must be used consistently. Don't fall into the trap of too much talk and emotion: Lecturing, nagging, and arguing just don't work. Simply follow the program and give praise when tokens are earned.

30. Class Meetings

On a regular basis, take a few minutes to discuss the classroom atmosphere. Any perceived problems or concerns can be addressed. The students, with guidance from the teacher, need to be a part of the solution for various problems as they may arise. Students need to use "I" messages and stay away from blaming or impugning others. There are three general rules to follow when a problem arises. Talk about: 1) what happened; 2) how you feel; and 3) what you really want.

More Classroom Accommodations

It's the little things that often make the difference. We've found that a few seemingly minor classroom modifications can make the difference in helping the ADHD student to be successful. Here are several quick and easy accommodations.

31. Consider a Vibrating Watch as a Self-Monitoring Tool

There is a watch available, which can be set at designated intervals, to vibrate and help one refocus. Address is: L&S&S Group Inc., P.O. Box 673, Northbrook, IL. The watch is also available through A.D.D. Warehouse.

32. C. O. R. Directions

Provide clear directions.

- Establish eye Contact
- Give One direction at a time (avoid multiple commands)
- Have student Repeat directions

33. Homework Folder Technique

Use assignment sheet and folder with pockets.

- In one pocket the student keeps an assignment log on a sheet of paper or premade form (see page 27 for an example). As assignments are given, the student records each assignment and puts the sheet back in the pocket of the folder.

- As each homework assignment is completed, it is placed in the other pocket of the folder. All completed assignments are kept in the folder which is taken to all classes. (Completed work can be color-coded with a marker to organize assignments.)

34. Bite-Sized Tasks

Break up lengthy assignments into bite-sized portions. Assist students in setting up realistic intermediate goals. Provide short breaks as goals are met.

35. Reduce Load

Reduce the length of assignments and tasks. Instead of requiring all items to be done, require only a portion to be finished. For example, ten math problems done well is better than the ADHD child feeling overwhelmed with 30 problems, and not trying. The goal, of course, is to gradually increase the amount of work performed.

36. Extra Time

Provide extra time to complete tasks. On tests or classwork, the ADHD student may need more time. While the student should work on increasing the pace, extra time to complete tasks may take off pressure. Quality work and completing tasks are the goals.

37. Frequent Monitoring

Monitor students frequently. ADHD students require more attention by the teacher to stay on task. Proximity to students and unobtrusive cuing are helpful (see page 46).

38. Predictable, Placid, Positive Discipline

Consistently follow pre-established rules and consequences:

- Display and remind students of classroom rules.

- Use a calm approach; each teacher should avoid too much emotion and discussion when disciplining students:
    Teachers do well to have their own emotion-reduction plan.
    Do not overreact to inappropriate behavior.

- Avoid sarcasm and ridicule.

39. Highlight Textbooks

Allow students to highlight old textbooks. This allows students to identify main points of information and provides an easier way to review information for tests. Ask the school to provide a 2nd set of books to the family, even if a deposit is required. This helps with forgetfulness.

40. Alternate Methods

Use a tape recorder, computer, and oral reports as alternative methods. Many students have trouble getting ideas down on paper. Alternative learning devices and methods help students to acquire important information and to show what they have learned. Devices also help to hold attention longer. We recommend utilizing books on tape for students who struggle with reading. A good source for text books on tape is Recording for the Blind and Dyslexic (RFB&D). For more information, call 1-800-803-7201.

41. Ounce of Prevention for Transitions

Give clear directions and provide extra supervision for these students during transition times. Time between classes and activities are likely times for trouble. Recess is another problematic time. Planned or structured activities prevent discipline problems. Constant proximity to an adult in charge may be necessary.

42. Clothespin Method

The teacher wears a clothespin when it is time to be quiet. No questions (except in cases of emergencies) are asked during these times. The clothespin is simply a cue to the students to work independently. Other cues signaling a time for independent work may include wearing a sticker, lights out, use of a timer, etc.

43. Exercise

Provide opportunities to briefly exercise. All students need to get pent up energy out and to get refreshed. It is not easy to sit for long periods of time. Another benefit of exercise is that it reoxygenates the brain and increases glucose. Don't forget to encourage students to drink lots of water. One of the first signs of distraction is dehydration.

44. Appropriate Fiddling

Allow the student to "fiddle" in a way that does not interrupt the learning process (i.e., squeezing a stress ball, quietly tapping knee, doodling, etc.). The student can be creative in figuring out ways to get out pent up energy. The teacher and student can agree upon an unobtrusive form of relieving stress and energy.

45. Internal Locus of Control

Include child in plans to cope with ADHD. Children have a wonderful ability to work out problems in their lives. Too often these students tend to have an "external locus of control" (others control me). Instead, they need to acquire an "internal locus of control" (I control myself). ADHD students need to be part of the solution and take responsibility for behavior that can be controlled.

46. Visual Aids

Write or post a daily schedule and assignments in the same place each day. Students who see what is going to be happening or what needs to be done can keep track of their progress.

47. Clutter-Free Handouts

Use clear, uncluttered handouts. Less information on a page that is well organized promotes easier learning. Use graph paper for math assignments. This helps with organizing math problems easier.

48. Mind Mapping

A method to stimulate a student's prior knowledge of a topic is called mind mapping. These maps are graphic diagrams developed by the student to order the information heard. Students write down key words and draw connecting lines to make an illustration that summarizes key points so that the outline can be more easily remembered (Polloway and Patton, 1989).

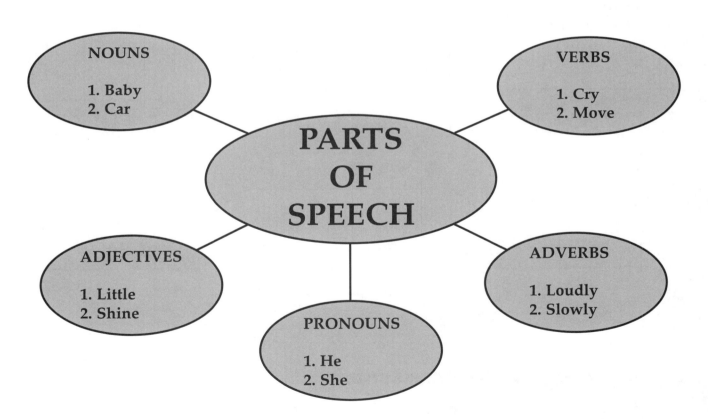

49. Multiple Intelligence

Help students find how they are smart. In our schools nationwide, school success has largely been based on the verbal and mathematical skills of the student. Dr. Howard Gardner, from Harvard University, has done extensive research on his theory of multiple intelligence. Dr. Gardner theorizes that there are seven important types of intelligence, as outlined in the diagram below.

The reason it is important for students, parents, and educators to support the Gardner Theory is that a strong self-esteem is largely based on the belief that everyone is talented and valued in some area of their intellectual being (Gardner, 1983). Students with ADHD, who may not consistently score high in the verbal or math areas, tend to believe that they are "slow" and "less capable" of setting and meeting goals. By introducing these students to Dr. Gardner's theory, they can hopefully reevaluate the importance of each of the other five intelligences to recognize their strengths.

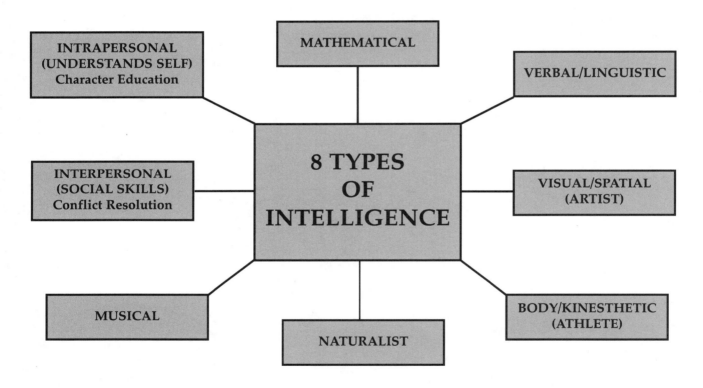

50. Learning Style Assessment

Student learning modalities have been researched by Milton Erickson. He believes the head and eye movements used by students, when questions are asked of them, provide us with important clues.

Ask questions such as:

- What significant event happened in your life a year ago?

- What significant event is happening now?

- What do you hope will happen a year from now?

If eye movements are to the side and head turned, the auditory mode may be strong. If eyes and head drop, the feeling, kinesthetic mode may be strong.

Remember that teachers tend to teach through their own learning styles. Don't forget to be observant and stress all of the senses.

Handling Oppositional Defiant Behavior

ADHD children and adolescents and oppositional defiant behavior often go together. Impulsive behavior and a seeming inability to follow directions can create an "I'm bad" mentality. Frustration and anger can become constant feelings. Unhappy people tend to be difficult. Handling negative behaviors and attitudes in constructive ways is imperative to avoid driving a wedge between adults and children. The following are ideas to proactively deal with misbehavior and hopefully win over the child or adolescent.

51. Weighing Misbehavior

Distinguish between **incompetence** versus **noncompliance**. An inability to do what is asked or required is far different from willful misbehavior. Punishing incompetence will only provoke anger in the child or adolescent. Patience and training go a long way in encouraging improved work or behavior.

52. Cause Catching

Look for the underlying causes of behavior. Adlerians believe behavior is purposeful. Four common reasons behind behaviors include:

a. Trying to gain **power** or control

b. **Revenge** or getting even

c. Trying to get **attention**

d. **Inadequate feelings** or low self-esteem

53. Family Counseling

Families are greatly affected when a member has ADHD. It is not uncommon for the child or adolescent who has ADHD to get the label of "bad." The person with ADHD can become the scapegoat or get the blame for family problems. Family counseling helps everyone in the family to change and act more constructively. As each member understands their situation and takes responsibility for his/her issues, life can get better. The co-dependent trap of overfunctioning and centering life around the ADHD child is avoided.

54. Appealing

Communicate, "You're an important part of this family or class. We need you." Let the ADHD child know that you care and that you'll get through this together. Building rapport and enlisting the help of the child or adolescent is paramount to success.

55. Adolescent Partnership

Work on a partnership for independence vs. an adversarial relationship. The relationship must become more adult to adult.

Key adolescent issues for adults to understand include:

    a. conformity - wanting to fit in

    b. searching for own identity (detaching from parents)

    c. generation gap - psychological moratorium (developing own values and beliefs)

    d. puberty - growth, body changes, sexuality

    e. inferiority - common feelings of inferiority when compared to others

56. Intervention Technique

For more serious behavioral problems, school officials or parents may want to use the "intervention technique." This technique is explained in detail in the book *Choices and Consequences* (Schafer, 1987). This book provides a step-by-step system of dealing with severe behavior problems. The focus is mostly on what to do when a teenager uses alcohol or other drugs. The following is an example of an intervention form that was developed and an explanation.

Intervention

An "intervention session" by concerned persons is done by presenting data or facts on inappropriate behavior. Each person documents actual events, beginning with the oldest and ending with the most recent. These happenings may cover several years. This is done to show that the student's inappropriate behavior didn't just begin last week but has actually been a problem for some time.

- Data should be based on events or behavior which you have witnessed or are sure actually happened. (Example: "Dave, last Saturday night you came home drunk. You were so drunk you tripped and fell at the door. You argued with everybody, slurred your words, and staggered around the house. Then you passed out on the couch and stayed there the remainder of the night. You do not act like that when you're not drinking. I said nothing to you, but I felt hurt and extremely disappointed.")

- Data should include harmful behavior and actual consumption whenever possible. "Son, you keep alcohol hidden in your room and car. Two weeks in a row last month, you also drank two bottles of gin from the family liquor supply."

- Data should be presented with care and concern. "I am here because I love and care about you and I want you to get well. You promised to stop drinking before, but after a short period, you have always started again. It has gotten worse. I care about you and I want you to get help."

- Data should point out contradictions in values and behavior which occur when they exhibit the unwanted behavior "Dave, you have been a good student and have even made the honor roll several times. You also have been known for good behavior and politeness. Last month I received five complaints about your being rude. This isn't like you." Or, "You are a good kid and have always treated me with respect. On the Fourth of July, you hit me. You never hit me before and would never hit me if you were thinking clearly. You've changed."

Use the following sheet marked "Documentation Sheet" to list your data. You may use additional paper, if needed, but use the same headings.

Name _____

Documentation Sheet

Date	This is what happened	This is what I did (and said)	This is how I feel

57. Emotion-Reduction Plan

Parents and teachers need to use their own emotion-reduction plan. Have a few activities or ways to reduce your stress (i.e. positive self-talk, exercise, etc.) Teaching and parenting is most stressful. We need to take good care of ourselves by relieving stress in constructive ways daily. Above all, don't get caught up in a power struggle. Avoid arguments and stick with your discipline plans.

58. Option Offering

Allow simple alternatives whenever possible to diffuse a tense situation. For example, state, "I am not going to argue about this. You have a choice. You and I can work this out or you can settle it with the principal." In this way, the burden is taken off the adult. The student is helped to make a better choice.

59. Major on Majors

Have only a **few** rules but make them hard and fast with clear cut consequences. When the student chooses to break rules, he/she gets him/herself into trouble. The rules have been pre-established and are commonly known.

60. Feeling Tone

Provide regular opportunities to interact with you. Explain your interest in the student's feelings and compromise whenever possible. Listen to the child's point of view. A good rule of thumb is that the answer is always "yes" unless there is a good reason to say "no." Adults admitting their mistakes show humility which is respected and appreciated.

61. Verbal Interventions

When a student is emotionally upset and aggressive behavior is possible, the following verbal intervention can help to diffuse the situation.

- Give clear, concise directions.
- Use a calm voice.
- Use a slow cadence if child is angry.
- Set clear limits.
- Use humor whenever possible.
- Use simple language.
- Speak respectfully with nonjudgmental words.
- Give positive choices.

62. Empathic Listening

The book, *How To Talk So Kids Will Listen and Listen So Kids Will Talk* (Faber and Mazlish, 1982), wonderfully demonstrates how important it is to really communicate with children. Good communication skills bring about cooperation, thus reducing conflict. The following are a few keys to good communication with children.

- Listen to understand the child's point of view.

- Give undivided attention.

- Focus on feelings of the child.

- Restate what the child is saying (summarize and clarify).

- Use simple acknowledgements (nod head, say uh-huh, etc.).

63. Proxemics

Standing in a nonthreatening way is necessary when there is potential for aggressive behavior. If the child is agitated:

- Respect personal space (at least 1 1/2 to 3 feet).

- Stand sideways (less threatening and less vulnerable).

64. Management-Miscue Avoidance

Avoiding common pitfalls disciplining children takes a conscious effort. Parents, in general, have a tendency to make certain mistakes when children misbehave. When made aware of these mistakes, common pitfalls can be avoided. We have identified a few of these common mistakes.

a. Nagging and Too Much Talk

Many parents tend to use far too much nagging. Somehow we think our best lectures will pay off. In reality, children have heard it all before and conveniently tune adults out. When our three part sermons don't work, the adults often turn to nagging. This effort typically pushes children toward passive-aggressive behavior. They intentionally don't do what the adult wants them to do.

b. Too Much Distress

With all the talk not working, parents' distress is certain to increase. When too much stress is involved, the potential for abuse, be it verbal or physical, increases. Arguing typically occurs at this stage. Yelling can turn into hitting.

- **Ineffective Cycle** - At best, too much talk and too much distress are ineffective. At worst, it is emotionally and/or physically abusive. Reasoning, persuading and begging leads to frustration causing arguing and yelling. Shouting matches may eventually lead to hitting.

The escalating cycle looks like this.

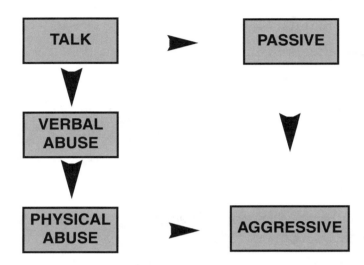

c. Seeking Approval

Many adults try to get their children to like them. Children, and for that matter, adolescents, tend to be fickle. One minute they like the adult, and the next minute they don't. Kids will eventually grow to appreciate adults who are consistent and fair. This also brings about feelings of security.

d. Expecting Children to Be Little Adults

Too often, adults expect children to be reasonable and unselfish. In a child's egocentric state, this is a lot to expect. Actions truly speak louder than words. Appropriate consequences do much better in shaping up positive behavior.

e. Ineffective Communication

- *Nonspecific directions* - The adult says vague things such as, "You're going to get in trouble," or "Be good."

- *Information overload* - The adult gives multiple directions. Several commands are given at once such as, "Clean your room, put your bike away, and feed the dog." This is simply overwhelming to the ADHD child.

- *Fuzzy commands* - The adult again is unclear about who and what. For example, "Let's do your homework now," or "Are you ready to do your homework?" These commands are confusing. In the first case, it is implied that the adult will help. In the second, it is implied that the child can opt to say no.

f. Not Following Through

Adults who delay and inconsistently dish out consequences for noncompliance run the risk of reinforcing negative behaviors. Immediate and consistent consequences are needed. A time limit of only a few seconds for compliance is recommended.

65. Understanding Manipulation

We've identified five common types of manipulation which adults need to recognize to make sure they are not being played "out foxed". Manipulation is any attempt by the child or adolescent to control the adult.

a. Badgering

The child constantly asks, whines, and pesters to get what he/she wants. He/she won't take no for an answer.

b. Intimidation

The child engages in temper tantrums, screaming, and arguing.

c. Threatening

The child says things like, "I'm going to run away," or "I'll just kill myself." While it is a good idea to supervise a child who says things like these to make sure he/she doesn't impulsively do something dangerous, usually he/she is simply trying to control the adult involved.

d. Martyrdom

The child plays the "woe is me" role. "No one likes me," or "I never get to do anything" are common lines.

e. Aggression

Some children display anger and even physically attack. More common is passive-aggressive behavior. Passive-aggressive behavior involves a general non-compliance and uncooperativeness. Intentionally not being on time, giving the least possible effort, and not talking are examples of this type of behavior.

Approaches to Discipline

There is, of course, no "cookie cutter" approach to discipline that always works. Children and adolescents are all different in the way they respond to various discipline techniques. Finding what works for a particular child or adolescent takes time and effort. Here are some approaches that are often effective.

66. Natural Consequences

These are consequences that allow children to live with the results of what they've done. For example, if a child gets his new bike covered with mud, he/she must clean it thoroughly before it can be used again. Another example might be a child losing a favorite toy. It is not replaced unless he/she earns enough money to purchase another one. The goal is not to rescue the person. Instead, he/she is faced with the results of what has been done.

67. Logical Consequences

Certain actions are taken that fit what the child has done. The adults in charge do this because they believe they will teach a lesson. For example, if a teenager breaks his/her curfew, he/she is grounded the next day. Another case might involve a child riding a bike repeatedly without a helmet. The bike is then taken away for a period of time.

68. Behavior Modification

The most effective program we've seen is the *1-2-3 Magic* Program developed by Dr. Thomas Phelan (1984). This program is very systematic and easy to implement. It is geared for children ages 3-12. Very basic behavioral techniques are used to stop negative behaviors and start positive behaviors. The video tape or book detailing this program can be ordered by calling 1-800-44 CHILD.

Behavior modification centers around the use of reinforcers and consequences.

Reinforcers include:

- *Providing praise* - verbal acknowledgments of positive behavior.

- *Using privileges* - rewards that afford certain activities (TV, outdoor play, trip to park, etc.) for positive behavior.

- *Providing tangibles* - material rewards for positive behavior.

Consequences include:

- *Losing privileges.*

- *Using restriction/grounding.*

- *Using time-out.*

69. Charting

Make a chart which clearly helps the child to see what behaviors need improvement. The chart will serve as a daily visual reminder of behavioral objectives. The child can help identify specific goals. Meet with the child to list expectations. Child and parent mark the chart each day with checks, stars, stickers, etc. when behavior standards are met. Select a reward and a certain amount of points for the reward. Gradually increase the number of points needed as child earns rewards.

70. Improving a Specific Behavior

Focus on only one behavior. List the specific goal and work out a regular schedule to evaluate progress. Set goal reasonably low to encourage success. For example, the student may be trying to turn in assignments on time. A reward may be given for every three tasks completed. This number will increase gradually so more work is needed to earn the reward. Increase the number of points needed as rewards are earned.

71. Contracting

Putting an agreement in writing formalizes a plan for improvement. The three keys are as follows:

- Decide what the child and parent(s) agree to do.
- Set a time frame.
- Choose a reward the child really wants (see Reinforcement Inventory on page 23).

72. Family or Class Meetings

Resolving or managing problems as they arise is wise. Families and classrooms that have open communication and problem solving tend to be healthier systems. Use the guidelines that follow.

- Have regular times for meetings.
- Keep a running list of concerns to be discussed at meetings.
- Interrupting is not allowed.
- Use "I" messages ("I feel" or "I think").
- Avoid judging, blaming, shaming, ridiculing, or name calling.

73. Parent Pitfall-Proofing

Parent Pitfalls to Avoid

Being a parent is a very tough job! Parents not only face the financial obligations of raising their children, but they deal with the guilt that their personal responsibilities might take away time from those they love. Because many kids today have a lot of unsupervised time, there are many opportunities for them to make choices that they may be unprepared to make. Although kids may try to make their parents think they are the "only" parents who claim the role of "boss" by setting firm limits, that ploy is just not true! In order to avoid some of the common parental pitfalls of enabling kids to be "at risk" of making poor choices in life, consider the following illustration.

Mind ⇨ Emotions ⇨ Behavior

Think of your mind, emotions, and behavior as being like a small train. Notice your mind is the engine that drives the train. Your emotions and behavior follow behind. Since your mind is the engine, it is important to feel in control. Set fair parental rules with which you are comfortable, then consistently stand firm. (Consider Canter's *Assertive Discipline (1982)* and Phelan's *1-2-3 Magic* (1984). Don't fall into a trap of believing some of the following misconceptions about kids:

Mind pitfalls that contribute to parental enabling:

- "I can't expect my child to be responsible."
- "He/she doesn't listen to me anyway."
- "My child tells me all the other kids are allowed to go."
- "If I really love my child, I should always trust him/her."

Based on what your mind is thinking, a range of emotions will follow behind. If your mind is filled with doubts about the job you're doing in rearing your child, negative feelings will most likely be present. It is important to try and achieve a healthy balance between trusting and setting parental boundaries for kids. Remember, kids cannot raise themselves. They need parents to guide them even if at the time there is disappointment.

Emotional pitfalls to avoid so children aren't running the household or feeling helpless:

- The parent is overly protective and unwilling to give the child opportunities to learn how to make good decisions.

- The parent doubts their ability to set household rules that are fair.

- The parent has a fear of losing a child's love and hearing phrases such as: "I'm not going to listen," "I hate you," "I don't care what you think," and "I don't have any friends because of you."

- The parent feels too much anxiety over child's performance and tends to over-structure their child's time, make comparisons to siblings too frequently, or expect the child to grow up too quickly.

Because of the way we think and feel, behaviors are created. Although everyone makes mistakes, as parents we must avoid pitfalls that actually make problems worse in the long run. Try to present yourself in a loving but assertive manner.

Behavioral pitfalls to avoid:

- Parents should not ignore inappropriate behavior just because they are tired or fed up.

- Parents should not give in or back down on a rule just because they want to avoid a conflict or are disappointed.

- Parents should not do their child's work because of fear that their child will fail if left to stand on his/her own two feet.

- Parents should not, as a rule, keep secrets from the other parent or caregiver. Kids will learn to play one parent against the other.

- Parents should not cover up for a child's mistakes.

- Parents should not set unrealistic expectations.

Being aware of these common parental pitfalls, the day-to-day job of raising children can be less frustrating and much more gratifying. You are the parent at your home, and it is quite acceptable to have rules for those who live there.

Improving Communication with ADHD Children

Adults are accustomed to talking to, and teaching children. This pedagogical relationship is necessary for training children about important matters that need to be learned in order to be successful in life. However, adults often neglect to really listen to their children. Like adults, children need to express feelings and thoughts and know that they are being heard. This is vital for self-esteem and relationship building. The rule of thumb is to listen to your child in just the same way you would listen to your boss, colleague, or friend. Here are a few tips for good communication with children and people in general.

74. Regular Check-In

The times adults spend directly interacting with children can typically be measured in minutes if not seconds. Being involved and frequent communication are earmarks of healthy families. A few suggestions follow:

- Be available to talk when the child needs to discuss a matter. Look for teachable moments.

- Choose a time when there are few distractions.

- Plan regular times to just talk about how things are going.

75. Plain Talk

Adults tend to talk "over the heads" of children, who may not pick up on subtleties such as humor or big words. Keep in mind that children have a shorter attention span.

- Use simple, clear language.

- Keep discussion as brief as possible.

- Have child summarize what you've said to check understanding. For example, "Could you tell me what you think I said?"

- Pronounce words clearly. Don't mumble.

- Don't use sarcasm or exaggeration.

76. Attention Focusing

Get the child's full attention before giving directions. This reduces frustration and needless repetition.

- Call child by name.

- Get eye contact (stoop down to be at child's level if necessary).

- Touch child's shoulder or chin.

77. Nonverbal Communications

Watch voice tone and body language. Adults need to realize that communication goes beyond words. It's not what we say, it's how we say it.

- Tone of voice should be under control and appropriate to the situation (say what you mean and mean what you say).

- Communication is 55% body language, 38% voice tone, and 7% the words one uses.

78. Contacting

Sitting on the floor and getting on eye level with the child sends a positive message. Adults are less imposing and more inviting when they are playful and at eye level. It's worth taking the time to have fun with children. It wins them over.

- Lean slightly forward.
- Use open body language (arms uncrossed).
- Use appropriate facial expression (smile, look of concern, etc.).
- Nod head gently from time to time.

79. Facilitative Responses

Listen, Listen, Listen! Showing kids that they are being heard is critical. While they don't need a lot of talk from adults, responding briefly and appropriately helps children tell the important things they want to communicate.

- Reflect feelings (I guess you feel_____about that.)

- Summarize and clarify what is being said. (Say what is being said in your own words. "So, you're saying...")

- Ask a few open questions (what, where, when or how).

- Avoid interrupting.

- Generally avoid giving advice, analyzing, supporting, and reassuring. (Communicate that you respect the child's ability to handle the situation.

Section 3

ESTABLISHING PATTERNS OF SUCCESS: COPING SKILLS FOR ADHD CHILDREN AND ADOLESCENTS

Children and adolescents with ADHD need coping skills. Even if a person takes medication as prescribed for ADHD, typically this isn't enough. They still need to learn how to study and concentrate, how to develop good relationships with peers, how to control impulses, and even how to feel good about themselves. These are learned skills that need to be taught. This section offers a collection of ideas that can be imparted to children and adolescents in a practical manner.

Study Skills

ADHD children and adolescents in general need two things when it comes to improving their academic fortunes: They must work **harder** and **smarter**. As students learn better and faster ways to study, they naturally get more motivated. The following are proven study tips which we call "the big ten."

80. Pace

Students are encouraged to estimate how long a task should take. Teachers can help students set time goals. The students work to stay on task and finish their task in the time allotted. Students are cautioned to not rush through their work, but to move steadily ahead.

81. Bracket

Students can strengthen their abilities to block out of their minds external distractions (sights and sounds around them) and internal distractions (thoughts and feelings). The power of concentration improves with practice.

82. Study Time

A specific time should be set aside each day for homework and studying. At least one hour should be devoted to completing assignments, studying for tests, and working on long-term projects. This daily practice builds self-discipline and reinforces information and skills (see page 38).

83. Study Place

Everyone needs a good place to study. This place needs to be well planned so that it is quiet, well lighted, and has all necessary materials within easy reach. Include supplies such as pencils, pens, glue, tape, scissors, markers, etc.

84. Organization

Teach students that everything has a place. Organize books and notebooks daily in the same order in desks and lockers. Use a three-ring notebook and use dividers for each subject. Have plenty of papers in each section in order to take good notes. Also, each day clean out all papers and debris that are not needed from the backpack, desk, and notebook (see page 25).

85. Proofread

Encourage students to check over their work for careless mistakes before handing in an assignment or test. Students should check for errors in spelling, punctuation, grammar, and math computation.

86. Follow Directions

Before beginning a task, teach students to read all directions. If the directions are not clearly understood, students need to learn to ask for clarification. Students need to learn to follow all directions in the given order (see page 31).

87. Homework Folder

Write down all assignments on a paper or homework sheet. Keep this sheet in one of the pockets of the homework folder. All completed assignments are kept in the other pocket so they will all be in the same location and easily retrieved when they are due (see pages 27 - 30).

88. Listen with Your Whole Body

Teach students to sit up tall and look at the speaker. Also, teach the students how to "read the teacher's mind." This is done by observing the teacher's nonverbal behavior. Look for:

- gestures
- facial expressions
- voice tone, cadence, and volume
- eye contact
- feelings being expressed

All of these give clues as to what is really important to the teacher and likely to be on the test.

89. Participate

Teach students to be involved with the lesson by asking good questions and answering questions. Students should attempt to write the important ideas in their notes. An added benefit of participating is that time does move along much faster.

90. Student Request Accommodations

Teachers and students do well to work together. Students with ADHD should be actively involved in being a part of the learning solution. An informal or formal plan for classroom modification should be discussed. Earlier in this book a great number of accommodations were listed. Here are a few that have worked well for many students. Make the following suggestions to the student:

a. **Change your seat to a quiet area**. For example:

  1. Sit up front with your back to the rest of the class to keep other students out of view.

  2. Sit near the teacher's desk.

  3. Sit away from doors, windows, and air conditioners if possible.

  4. Sit near a serious student who works hard and doesn't bother others.

b. **Request a "study pal."** (Sitting near a classmate who is a good student can help. This person can remind you to get back on task and can answer questions you may have.)

c. **Request extra time to complete assigned work.**

d. **Request shortened assignments.** (Try to do more and more as you improve.)

e. **Set a time limit for classwork to be done using a kitchen timer.**

f. **Establish a private signal that your teacher can use to remind you to get back on task.** (Example: A tap on the shoulder or a secret code word such as "BOT," which means get Back On Task.) See page 46, "Cuing Strategy" for more ideas of private signals you and your teacher may use.

g. **Start a system where the teacher asks you to repeat directions.** This ensures the teacher that the directions are understood before beginning an activity or assignment.

h. **Check desk and notebook for neatness and content.** You are accountable to keep up with notes and assignments.

i. **Have your teacher sign your assignment pad at end of day to make sure your assignments are written down correctly.**

(Frank and Smith, 1994)

91. SQ3R

An age-old method for reading better and faster is called SQ3R. Teach the following steps to students and encourage them to practice, practice, practice. As this system becomes a habit, two benefits should emerge: An increase in speed by making reading more efficient, and improved comprehension.

Survey   Quickly look over the assignment. Skim over the pages assigned and get an idea of what it is about. This should take less than a minute.

Question   Look carefully at the questions at the end of the section which you will likely need to do for homework. Also look at the headings and try to turn them into questions.

Example: Heading - School in Colonial Days

Question - What was school like in Colonial Days?

Read   Read to answer the questions. This is called scanning. This means you are just looking for the answers to questions and main ideas.

Write   Take notes. Write down the answers to the questions and take a few notes on the main ideas.

Review   Before you stop, take a minute to think about what you've learned. Look over your notes and quiz yourself.

(Frank and Smith, 1994)

Concentration/Listening

Concentration and listening are skills. These skills need to be taught and practiced. Far too often we tell kids to listen or pay attention, but they have never been formally taught how. Here are two ideas to aid listening and concentration.

92. Systematic Listening and Concentration

Whether it's getting more out of each lesson or following through on tasks to their completion, this five-step skill has proven to be effective. It enhances one's power of concentration by getting students to think about what they need to do for success. We call it "Systematic Listening and Concentration."

Step 1: Refocus   Teach students to put aside whatever they are doing and start thinking about the lesson or activity at hand. Get out necessary materials and look over past notes or readings.

Step 2: Pay Attention   Teach students to pay attention to all distractions that might get in the way of the lesson or activity. Notice internal distractions (feelings and thoughts such as being hungry, tired, angry, etc.), and external distractions (sights and sounds around us such as a glare from the sun or a light buzzing).

Step 3: Bracket   Consciously teach students to block these distractions out of their minds. A commitment or promise is needed to think only about the present task.

Step 4: Set Goal(s)   Help students set goals before the lesson or activity starts. Goals may include:

     a. Taking notes.

     b. Participating (Answering or asking at least so many questions).

     c. Trying to read the teacher's mind as explained before on page 76, actively listening and paying attention to non-verbal cues.

Step 5: Stay on Task   Remind students that they need to be on task or to maintain their concentration throughout the lesson or task. If daydreaming happens, remind students to bracket again.

An easy way to remember these five steps is to memorize the following silly sentence. "Ralph ate blue gummy toads." Each word stands for one of the five steps.

Ralph   =   Refocus

Ate   =   Attention

Blue   =   Bracket

Gummy   =   Goal(s)

Toads   =   Task

Before a lesson or task, students are asked to say the silly sentence to themselves and to think about each of the five steps. As they think about these steps prior to, and during lessons and activities, the students will become more focused. After many days of practicing these steps, they become automatic and increasingly more effective.

93. Beat the Clock

Another way to help students concentrate and stay on task is to play a simple game. With each assignment (classwork or homework), the student tries to guess how much time will be needed to finish. At first a teacher or parent may need to help the student judge how much time the work will likely take. A kitchen timer is then set with the number of minutes guessed. If there is no kitchen timer, simply figure by using a watch or clock when the task needs to be finished. Caution: Please allow a little extra time so students do not rush through the work. As students work steadily, they will find that they can beat the clock often.

(Frank and Smith, 1994)

Controlling Behavior

Being in control requires an ability to stop and make a good choice. Wisdom is often the ability to pause and consider what is the right or best thing to do. ADHD students need to learn to give themselves permission to think before acting. This, hopefully can become a good habit.

94. Head and Heart Impulse Control

Helping children and adolescents who have ADHD think before they act is not an easy job, however, it can be done. People with ADHD can learn to give themselves permission to think before doing. This is a habit that can be learned through much practice.

We teach children that they have two wonderful resources that can give them victory over impulsive behaviors that lead to certain trouble and danger. These two resources which need to be utilized are the **head** and **heart**.

Using Your Head

Teach kids to memorize three important questions. These questions are to be contemplated before a choice or action is taken. Children are asked to write down these three questions on an index card and to carry it with them in a pocket as a reminder to stop and think about what they are doing.

Students ask themselves:

1. What am I getting ready to do?

2. What will happen if I do this?

3. What can I do instead?

These three written questions become a "control card." It is a constant cue or reminder to engage the brain first.

Using Your Heart

The second resource is the heart. Ask students to memorize a promise of the *Just Say No Club*. Promise #4 reads, "If I ever have a scared, uncomfortable feeling inside about doing something, I'll just say no."

Students again are instructed to first pay attention to their heart or conscience before making a choice or taking an action. Students are encouraged to listen to their heart or conscience and think about doing the right thing.

Taking time to use the head and heart is wise. The split second it takes to think clearly and to notice one's feelings can make the difference in getting along or not.

Adapted with permission (Frank and Smith, 1994).

Self-Esteem

Most of the students we interviewed expressed negative feelings about themselves. While self-esteem is largely something one has to do for oneself, children and adolescents can be helped to think more constructively. One thing we can always control is our attitude. Negative thoughts have to change in order to improve self-esteem.

95. Clear Messages

So many children and adolescents who have ADHD feel inadequate. Self-esteem comes largely from thought patterns. Getting children to carefully evaluate thoughts and to confront negative thinking is a key to improving self-esteem.

Put in simple terms, try to get children to look at their self-talk. Essentially, people are giving themselves "clear messages" or "muddy messages." Muddy messages are thoughts that cause people to not feel good about themselves. When things bother us and we don't like ourselves, muddy messages are being sent. This obviously is nonproductive.

On the other hand, clear messages are thoughts that help people feel good about themselves and handle whatever comes their way. When clear messages are sent, people are more at peace and situations or circumstances don't bother us for long. We need to be more like a thermostat which sets the emotional climate versus a thermometer, which merely reacts to the conditions around it.

Here are some examples of clear versus muddy thinking.

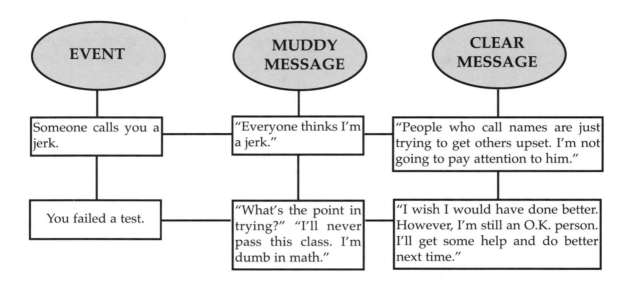

Some examples of clear messages are:

"I'm O.K."

"I can handle it."

"I'll just do my best."

"No one is perfect."

"It's going to work out."

(Frank and Smith, 1994)

Encourage children to replace muddy messages with clear messages. Have them say or list clear messages regularly. How people look at life is critical. It's a matter of perspective. Children need help to look at life both accurately and positively.

96. RASing Feelings

Feelings, like our bodies, need exercise. ADHD children seem to get frustrated and discouraged often. If taught to handle feelings well, feelings lose their power or hold over us. Teach children three steps to handling feelings. We call it "RAS."

R *means* **Recognize Your Feelings**.

Recognize means to know or to think about one's feelings. People have two types of feelings. Here are some examples of each type.

Pleasant Feelings		**Unpleasant Feelings**	
(Feelings we like to have.)		(Feelings we don't like to have.)	
happy	peaceful	sad	unhappy
excited	joyful	mad	worried
surprised	hopeful	upset	tired
warm	proud	frustrated	stupid
delighted	love	disappointed	nervous
friendly	confident	left out	scared
relaxed	content	guilty	embarrassed
included	respected	jealous	hurt

Recognizing or knowing what feelings a person has is very important. Throughout each day, teach children to stop for a minute and listen to their feelings. They can ask, "How am I feeling right now?" Their bodies and minds will tell them.

A *means* **Accept Your Feelings**.

Accept means that feelings are always O.K. Accept means to take feelings as they are. There is nothing wrong with feeling a certain way. Feelings are a part of being human, and they are O.K.

S *means* **Share Your Feelings**.

Feelings are to be **s**hared with others. Talking to people we trust about our feelings is a wonderful thing to do. Feelings are not to be kept inside. We just feel better when we talk to others about our feelings.

(Frank and Smith, 1994)

97. Chill Out Plan

The following is an exercise that we highly recommend when children and adolescents get angry. Kids with ADHD need to get a grip over anger and frustration. We can help them develop their personal "Chill Out Plans" so they'll have constructive ways to get over unpleasant feelings.

C.O.P.

To find a balance in our lives, it is a good idea to have a C.O.P. A C.O.P. is short for **Chill Out Plan**. This is a plan where one chooses a few healthy things to do when anger arises. Below is a list of ideas kids have shared that have helped them to get over their anger. Choose at least three or four things that you can do to chill out the next time you get angry. The more you use your C.O.P., the better you'll get at handling anger. Your C.O.P. will become automatic after a while, so practice, practice, practice.

Ideas for Chill Out Plan:

1. Talk to someone you trust.

2. Work out the conflicts conflict (talk out the problem with the other person as soon as possible).

3. Count to ten or higher to calm down.

4. Hit a pillow or punching bag.

5. Use positive self-talk (use of clear messages).

6. Walk away from arguments or teasing.

7. Squeeze a ball.

8. Read a book.

9. Pray about it.

10. Listen to music.

11. Exercise.

12. Get alone and scream.

13. Take a time out.

14. Take a deep breath.

15. Write in a journal.

16. Take a one-minute vacation. (While not in class, imagine going to a favorite spot or doing a favorite activity.)

17. Break craft sticks.

18. Enjoy a pet.

19. Draw or paint your feelings.

20. Write a letter (even if you don't send it)

Your Chill Out Plan:

List three to five ideas you can do to chill out when angry.

1.

2.

3.

4.

5.

(Frank and Smith, 1994)

Relationship Building

Making friends and keeping friends is a difficult process that takes a lot of energy and skill. It can be a scary, difficult process for many students who have an attention deficit disorder. Oftentimes these students do not recognize that they must be responsible for their part in making a friendship work.

98. The Friendship Model

In interviewing kids about the qualities of good friends, here are some of the characteristics that scored the highest.

- a good listener

- someone you trust

- a patient person

- someone who is flexible and doesn't get upset easily

- someone who takes turns and shares

- a kind person who has good manners

- someone who thinks before acting in a hurtful way

To simplify the process of how to start a friendship, the friendship model has been developed. This concrete example, based on four simple steps, can help kids understand what their role is, and then take responsibility for working through all of the steps.

Friendship Model

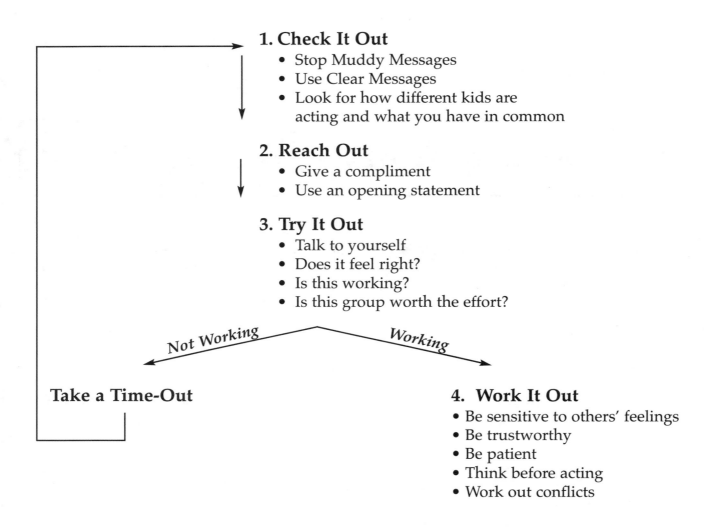

1. Check It Out
- Stop Muddy Messages
- Use Clear Messages
- Look for how different kids are acting and what you have in common

2. Reach Out
- Give a compliment
- Use an opening statement

3. Try It Out
- Talk to yourself
- Does it feel right?
- Is this working?
- Is this group worth the effort?

Not Working   *Working*

Take a Time-Out

4. Work It Out
- Be sensitive to others' feelings
- Be trustworthy
- Be patient
- Think before acting
- Work out conflicts

(Source: Smith and Walter, 1986)

Step 1: "Check it Out"

Everyone has a choice about the general mood of one's thinking. This thinking can be muddy (negative) or clear (positive). Thinking can either work for a person or against a person. Self-talk can make the difference between being liked by peers or rejected. For the most part, people enjoy being around individuals who are happy, kind, and unselfish. People have the power to control their thoughts, but thinking clear thoughts takes practice.

Also, kids need to know how to look for clear and muddy messages in other people. Clear messages are signs people send that attract others in a positive way. On the other hand, muddy messages show others that one is not acting like a friend. Students need to be taught to notice how others are behaving. This cues them about who might be a person to whom one can "reach out" and start a friendship. It goes without saying that the child with ADHD needs to keep his/her messages clear to be attractive to others.

Step 2: "Reach Out"

This step requires individuals to try to be friendly verbally and nonverbally. Verbally, the two easiest ways to reach out and start a conversation are with a compliment or by using an everyday statement. Teach children what is meant by a compliment and an everyday statement and practice them.

Teach the child:

A **compliment** is when you say something nice to someone, such as "I like your Tee-shirt," or "You are a good ball player."

An **everyday statement** is a sentence about almost anything, such as: "What is your favorite subject?," "Do you have any brothers or sisters?," "How old are you?," or "What movie is your all-time favorite?"

Another point to consider is teaching children how to nonverbally "reach out." Here are some examples of positive nonverbal communication.

- Smiling.
- Gaining eye contact.
- Using a pleasant voice tone.
- Keeping a comfortable distance from the person with whom you are speaking.
- Being neat and clean.
- Using good manners.

Step 3: "Try It Out."

When someone goes to the store to buy a pair of shoes, the person tries them on before buying them. The same idea goes with making friends. Children need to evaluate friendships. Students should consider the following questions:

- Do I feel comfortable being with them?

- Is it working?

- Does it feel O.K.?

- Do these people help me to be the best I can be?

This step involves deciding who a person's friends will be. If the answer to these questions is "no," friendships are **not** working out, then students take a "Time-Out" and ask what is going wrong. The child begins by checking out his/her messages. The child must make sure clear messages are being sent. Then the child continues to look for others who are sending clear messages.

Step 4:   "Work It Out."

If the answer is "yes" to questions like the ones in step three, then step four follows. "Work It Out" means keeping the friendship going. Students need to develop the skills of how to resolve conflicts along with continuing to keep messages clear. Teaching students how to use "I" messages and how to compromise are important skills. Even the best of friends won't always agree, however, conflicts can be managed in a healthy way if both parties listen to each other and discuss three things:

- What happened?

- How do they feel?

- What do they really want?

Students are asked to memorize the four-step friendship model. Children and adolescents need to think about each step every time they are trying to make and keep friends. Working with a counselor, teacher, or parent while applying the four steps is helpful.

(Source: Smith and Walter, (1986)

Utilizing Resources

One overlooked skill is knowing where to find help and encouragement. "Ask and you shall receive." Help is available for the asking. The ADHD child can build self-esteem and confidence by finding helpful people and places.

99. Private Tutoring

Individualized lessons and study skills can be taught on a regular basis at school or with a private tutor. Students need to learn how to ask their teachers for help. If more help is needed, a regular tutor can be sought. This person needs to specialize in showing how to study. Good tutoring is often available at local universities and colleges.

100. Support Groups

In school and outside of school, it is common to find ADHD support groups. Students can find they are not alone and gain coping skills. Students should seek out their school counselors. Some communities have regular support groups and small group counseling. Groups such as CHADD (Children and Adults with Attention Deficit Disorders) can help people find support and good ideas.

101. Social Activities

One great way to learn to appropriately interact with peers is to get involved with supervised groups where common values and citizenship are taught and encouraged. It's fun, too. Students can look for groups like scouts, church, afterschool activities, etc.

102. Individualized Activities

Karate, weight lifting, swimming, music, art, and bowling are examples of activities that build self-discipline and self-confidence. Students need to look for activities that fit their interests and strengths. Individual activities typically work best for children with ADHD.

A Note from the Authors

"Reducing the Deficit" is an attempt to outline for parents and teachers a clear, concise understanding of what an attention disorder actually is and how it can be best treated, both medically and behaviorally. We hope that we have provided you with a series of ideas which will allow your child or student to feel informed, supported, and confident. It is important for every team member to take responsibility for the role they play in creating a successful learning environment. As mentioned earlier, ADHD is a condition that is not going to go away, however, through the use of the ideas and skills presented, weaknesses can be turned into strengths. We hope this book will help enable many kids to find success.

Good luck! We wish you success as you use these techniques with your students.

Kim "Tip" Frank, Ed.S., LPC
Susan J. Smith-Rex, Ed.D.

References

American Psychological Association (1995). *Diagnostic and Statistical Manual IV*. Washington, D.C.: Author.

Baren, M. (1994). *Hyperactivity and Attention Disorders in Children.* Sam Ramen, CA: The Health Information Network.

Barkley, R. A. (1995a). ADHD and IQ. *ADHD Report*, 3(2), 1.

Barkley, R. A. (1998). Prevalence of ADHD. *U.S. ADHD Report*, 6(2).

Bauermeister, J. J. (1995). ADD and Hispanic (Puerto Rican) children: Some thoughts and research findings. *Attention*, 2(1), 16-19.

Canter, L. (1982). *Assertive Discipline for Parents.* Santa Monica, CA: Canter and Associates.

CHADD (1988). *Attention Deficit Disorders: A Guide for Teachers*. Plantation, FL: Author

Deshler, D.D., Schumaker, J.B., & Leny, B.K. (1984). Academic and cognitive interventions for LD adolescents. *Journal of Learning Disabilities*, 17, 108-117.

Fabor, A. and Mazlish, E. (1982). *How to Talk So Kids Will Listen and Listen So Kids Will Talk.* New York: Avon Books.

Fernald, G.M. (1943). *Remedial Techniques in Basic School Subjects.* New York: McGraw-Hill.

Frank, T. & Smith, S. (1994). *Getting a Grip on ADD.* Minneapolis, MN: Educational Media Corp.

Gardner, H. (1993). *Frames of Mind*. New York: Basic Books.

Hallowell, E. M., & Raley, J. J. (1995). *Driven to Distraction.* New York: Simon & Schuster.

Latham, P.S. and Latham, P.H. (1982). *Attention Deficit Disorder and the Law: A Guide for Advocates.* Washington, D.C.: JKL Communications.

Klein, R. (1987). Prognosis of Attention Deficit Disorder. Management in Adolescents. *Pediatrics in Review*, 8, 216-223.

Parker, H.C. (1992). *Listen Look and Think: A Self-Regulation Program for Children.* Plantation, FL: Impact Publications, Inc.

Phelan, T.W. (1984). *1-2-3 Magic: Training Your Preschoolers and Preteens to Do What You Want.*

Gen Ellyn, IL: Child Management, Inc.

Polloway, E. A. & Patton, J.R. (1989). *Strategies for Teaching Learners With Special Needs*. New York: Macmillan Publishing Co.

Schafer, D. (1987). *Choices and Consequences*. Minneapolis, MN: Johnson Institute Books.

Smith, S.J. and Walter, G. (1986). *Four Steps to Making Friends*. Rock Hill, SC: Winthrop University.

Newsweek (1996, May 18). Mothers little helper. 51-56.

Weiner, H.S. & Smith, S. (1994). *Reading Skills Handbook*. Boston, MA: Houghton Mifflin Co.